Cases in

EUROPEAN
MARKETING

RICHARD LYNCH

**KOGAN
PAGE**

To accompany this book, the author has written a *Lecturer's Guide*. This valuable text offers suggestions on how the material in *Cases in European Marketing* can be used with students. In addition, the guide attempts to answer the questions posed at the end of each case.

The *Lecturer's Guide* is available from Kogan Page Ltd at the address mentioned below, ISBN 0 7494 1350 6

First published in 1993

Kogan Page Limited
120 Pentonville Road
London N1 9JN

© Aldersgate Consultancy Limited, 1993.

British Library Cataloguing in Publication Data
A CIP record for this book is available from the British Library.

ISBN 0 7494 1118 X

Typeset by BookEns Ltd, Baldock, Herts
Printed in England by Clays Ltd, St Ives plc

Contents

List of figures

List of Tables

For our knowledge is imperfect and our prophecy is imperfect; but when the perfect comes, the imperfect will pass away.

Acknowledgements

After lecturing, writing and consulting on Europe for over five years, I have built up a body of cases that explore the major issues. This book is my attempt to record some of this material. It represents several years of development. And it has benefited greatly from the input of the various colleagues and individuals who have worked with me over this time. All have contributed something: a word of advice, a new insight, an opportunity to present a case or lecture series. I acknowledge your real contributions to this book.

As with my earlier books, I record my thanks to the European Commission for permission to use data and material from their extensive work on Europe. I am also grateful to Enrico Congedo for data on Italian mobile telecommunications.

As I write, this book still remains to be pored over by my publishers, Kogan Page. I have no doubt that they will suggest sensible improvements and I thank them for that.

Above all, I am grateful to the many managers and students who have explored Europe with me over the last few years: amazed, amused, appalled, astonished, argumentative, aggressive, acquiescent and even approving. You are too many to list individually, but my thanks are no less warm to each of you for your contributions.

The text is being pieced together over Easter 1993 when my family and friends might expect to have seen a little more of me. I thank them for their patience and encouragement.

SPECIAL NOTE FOR EDUCATORS AND LECTURERS

To accompany this book, I have devised a separate text that comments on each case and, in some cases, describes in detail what happened next. The *Lecturers' Guide* is available from the publishers.

Richard Lynch
London

1
Introduction

Over the last 30 years, marketing in Europe has become more challenging and more complex. Whether we are managers or students, we can all benefit from being stretched by the experiences of other companies coping with the realities of the European Community (EC) or the uncertainties of Eastern Europe.

The objective of this book is to explore some of the real challenges that companies marketing across Europe have encountered in the last few years. Case studies that describe actual situations, even though they are occasionally disguised, are the ideal way to explore this task.

European marketing has certainly had its share of difficulties over the last few years.

1. Rupert Murdoch's publishing empire, News International, joined the German publisher, Burda, to launch an East German version of its highly successful UK newspaper, the *Sun*. The German version was called *Super! Zeitung* and started in 1991.[1] It folded one year later after its better-established German rivals outdid its mixture of bingo, sex and popular photo-journalism by launching their own versions.[2]

2. After spending 625 million ECU (US\$ 600 million) trying to develop and establish a new European standard for high definition television (HDTV), the European Commission is now likely to back down from its development and use the US-developed HDTV system.[3] As a result, the two major European consumer electronics companies, Philips (The Netherlands) and Thomson (France), must be wondering what value to put on their extensive investment in the same area.[4]

3. Most of Europe's large computer companies have moved into massive losses: IBM, Olivetti, Groupe Bull and Siemens/Nixdorf have all suffered from the global economic downturn, coupled with major structural changes in world computer markets.[5] The single Europe does not appear to have produced even the 'minor savings' predicted in the EC's own Cecchini Report.[6]

4. General Electric (US) has invested US\$310 million in Tungsram, its Hungarian lighting subsidiary, which it purchased in 1989. In spite of a 25 per cent cut in

the labour force, the Hungarian company was still making losses three years later.[7]

EUROPEAN MARKETING CASE STUDIES

These are all rather short case studies with reasonably clear issues and lessons for the future. Much of European marketing concerns business situations that:

- are more complex;

- reflect the greater diversity of European customers;

- concern inter-relationships with government and the European Commission;

- involve new competitors.

European case examples need to reflect this multi-faceted reality. As a consequence, the resolution of each case study may well need both the application of well-known marketing concepts and some knowledge of European markets. Some information is usually available with a little ingenuity. But, as I know from over 20 years in marketing, the solution is not always the neat, well-ordered outcome subsequently presented by consultants: markets are misread; competitors form unexpected alliances or joint ventures; the European Commission takes an unexpectedly obscure decision; national governments decide to protect their national interests. You will find all these situations in the case studies in the book.

SO, WHAT IS EUROPEAN MARKETING?

European marketing relates the basic principles of marketing to the specific issues of the Europe of the 1990s:

- the opportunities and problems of the single Europe;

- the implications of the Maastricht Treaty;

- the enlargement of the EC;

- the potential and difficulties of Eastern Europe.

As a working definition, Europe is defined as all those countries between the Atlantic Ocean in the west and the Ural Mountains in the east. Within this large geographic area, there is clearly a basic distinction to be drawn: we have Western Europe with its relatively high wealth and developed economies. Then there is Eastern Europe with a skilled workforce, significant natural resources, but 40 or more years of centrally-planned economic 'progress' that have left many people impoverished and living in dilapidated infrastructures. The cases in this book concentrate on Western Europe, partly because marketing is still underdeveloped further East, but also because the West itself holds so many marketing opportunities.

Marketing issues are the backbone of this book. European marketing can be seen as the application of basic marketing principles to European issues. One way of considering this process is to link the issues together, as in Figure 1.1. This case book then presents the complex interactions that exist between these areas, alongside some of the consequences for European marketing decision making.

While it would be inappropriate in a case book to treat facets of the subject in a structured sequence, all the cases have been selected and developed to explore specific issues. These are shown in Table 1.1.

REFERENCES

1. Snoddy, R (1991) 'Murdoch boosts eastern exposure', *Financial Times*, 12 November, p 30.
2. Reuters (1992) 'Tabloid folds as Murdoch quits', *Financial Times,* 25 July, p 3.
3. Hill, A (1993) 'Europe will follow US lead over high-definition TV', *Financial Times*, 19 February, p 16.
4. Mead, G (1993) 'Philips suspends plans to produce HDTV televisions', *Financial Times*, 1 February, p 19.
5. *Economist* (1993) 'What went wrong at IBM?', 16 January, p 23.
6. Cecchini, P. (1988) '1992: the benefits of a single market', Wildwood House, p 22.
7. Denton, N (1992) 'GE faces more losses at Hungarian plant', *Financial Times*, 9 September, p 26.

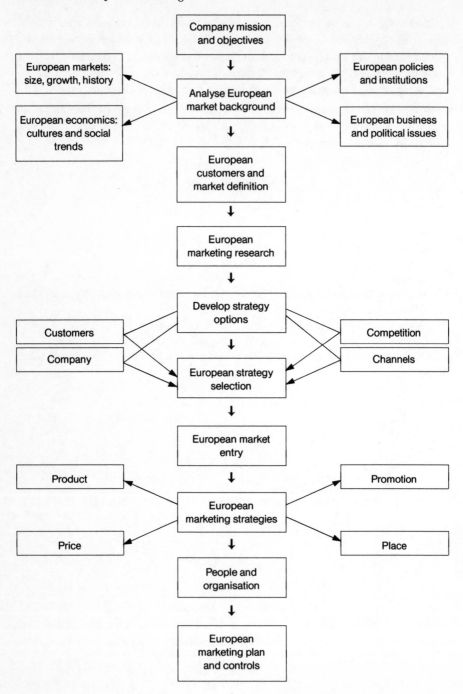

Figure 1.1 European marketing: decision-making process

Table 1.1 The cases and their links with European marketing issues

	Objectives	Political and economic factors	Customers	Marketing research	Strategy options	Strategy selection	Market entry	Product	Price	Promotion	Place	People
Computer software Products Inc	⊗											
Repsol	x	⊗	x				x				x	
BAT Tobacco	x	⊗	x		x		x					
Philips Whirlpool	x		⊗	⊗				x		x		
Courtauld's New 'Tencel' Fibre		x	x	⊗	x	x		x	x	x	x	
Irish Telephones	⊗	x	x	x	⊗			x	x	x	x	
European Breakfast Cereals			x	x	⊗	⊗	⊗	x	x	x	x	
North American entry strategies for Eastern Europe		⊗		x		x	⊗					
Jacobs Suchard	x				⊗	⊗	⊗	x	x	x	x	
European mobile cellular telephone network	⊗	⊗	x			⊗	⊗	x	x	x	x	
European car pricing	x		x					x	⊗			
AlpenFerien	x		x	x			x	x	x	x	x	
McDonalds			x				x	⊗	⊗	⊗	x	x
Electrolux							x	x			x	⊗
CMB Packaging					x	x						⊗

Key: ⊗ Major focus of case
  x Subject covered in case

2

European prospects for Computer Software Products Inc*

'We cannot be the only US company to be affected by the continuing European recession – our European sales revenue has fallen by over 10 per cent in the last year: labor costs have risen and we have been significantly affected by the downturn in the UK economy. The single European market of 1993 seems to have made little difference.'

James Kennedy, European sales manager for Computer Software Products Inc (CSP) was reviewing a difficult sales situation with his colleague, Robert Irwin, CSP's marketing manager for Europe. Kennedy continued: 'When I phoned the Commercial Section of the American Embassy in Brussels, they told me the USA has produced only a couple of simple leaflets on the European Community. All sales leads from US Embassies are produced on a country-by-country basis. We are just going to have to develop pan-European customers for ourselves.'

'We need to take a long hard look at our marketing in the European Community,' Irwin replied. 'The European Commission is predicting static economic growth across the EC in 1993. We have limited marketing resources and the EC has nearly 350 million people. There may even be better opportunities elsewhere in Europe. What about European Free Trade Area countries? Or even Eastern Europe?'

James Kennedy and Robert Irwin, senior managers at CSP, were discussing what to do about a short-term decline in sales to Europe. Since 1985, the company had been developing sales of specialised computer software to Europe. By 1989, it was selling a range of standard products as well as bespoke consultancy. Its customers were large and medium-sized companies across Europe. Total European sales in

1992 were US$ 15 million. Both the European subsidiary and the US parent company were trading profitably at this time.

Because ACP sales personnel primarily spoke English and were also most comfortable with British business practices, the company had concentrated on the UK, which accounted for around 70 per cent of European sales.

THE PRODUCT

CSP regarded itself as being at the forefront of product innovation in computer software. It had developed accounting software packages earlier than many companies, and then reconfigured these to run with local area networks and telecommunications networks. However, one of its problems recently, in both Europe and the USA, had been that some of the very large software houses had developed standardised packages that were essentially similar and rather cheaper.

In both the USA and Europe, CSP had therefore moved increasingly towards tailoring its standard software into individually designed solutions for large and medium-sized companies. As a result, it had been forced to recruit additional computer nationals in European countries such as the UK in order to produce bespoke solutions and service these customers. Standardised software packages now accounted for around 50 per cent of CSP total European sales.

SALES AND MARKETING

European sales were organised on a country basis with 18 salespeople in the UK, 4 in France and 5 in Germany. There were offices in London, Paris and Bonn. There were also five roving sales people who acted across Europe to pick up other sales leads or deal with companies having pan-European requirements that went beyond the three lead countries. Salespeople were then backed up by software design engineers with roughly two engineers per salesperson.

Salespeople were active in seeking sales contacts, understanding detailed customer requirements and then relaying these back so that an estimate could be made for either a software package or an individual design development. In the latter case, the acceptance of a bid from sales would trigger a process of briefing the CSP computer software engineers who would then spend time with clients developing and implementing the agreed solutions.

Marketing staff numbered eight in total and worked primarily out of the European headquarters at Slough near London. They undertook basic market analysis for the whole of Europe, developing new products and services. They also had responsibility for European marketing research and for promoting CSP beyond the existing customer base. Thus they organised mail shots, exhibitions, specialist advertising and sponsorship, etc.

For standard software products, marketing set the prices. For individual contracts, marketing also had a clearly defined responsibility to ensure that they were profitable: they therefore examined the estimates of the hours to complete the contract as quoted to the customer by the salesperson.

Essentially, the European marketing role was to look beyond the monthly sales opportunities of the sales team. Marketing concentrated on the totally new marketing opportunities: these came partly from new European customer trends, but also from exploiting developments already being marketed by CSP in the USA.

THE CURRENT SITUATION

Partly as a result of the European economic downturn, problems were beginning to emerge in CSP's European marketing and sales effort. Although the 'single Europe' had come into existence on 1 January 1993, the UK still accounted for a large part of total sales and European potential had not been fully exploited. This was both a problem and an opportunity.

With the opening up of Eastern European markets, CSP had also seen a couple of their competitors take the first steps into Poland, Hungary, and the Czech and Slovak Republics. There was clearly potential for major sales in the medium term, but the risks were also significant.

CASE QUESTIONS

1. How would you advise the company to approach European opportunities? Do they need to set themselves specific European marketing and sales objectives at this stage? If so, what might they be?

2. Does the company need to examine the economic prospects of individual countries or take Europe as a whole? What benefits, if any, are likely to be gained from the 'single Europe' by this company? If there are any, how might these be exploited?

3. How should the company approach the software markets of Eastern Europe?

3

Repsol: The barriers come down in Spanish petrol retailing*

This case study looks at three major oil companies, the single Europe and its impact on the Spanish market for oil and petrol:

- Repsol SA, Spain;

- Elf Aquitaine SA, France;

- British Petroleum, UK.

We start with some background on oil markets and the major oil companies in Europe. Single Europe barriers are then explored. Finally, the activities of each of the three companies is described in turn up to mid-1990 in the context of the Spanish oil and petrol market.

THE EUROPEAN OIL AND PETROL MARKET

Virtually all the major oil companies across Europe are engaged in the four principal oil industry activities of

- exploration for new wells;

- production of crude oil and gas;

- refining to meet specific customer requirements;

- distribution of products to customers.

Importantly, distribution means not only logistics but also the strategies necessary to secure channels of supply to customers. This case concentrates on distribution activities for the three companies above because:

- oil company strategy will partly be determined by the security of its distribution outlets; and
- refining and distribution are the parts located within the single Europe and thus particularly governed by changes up to 1993.

Since the oil crisis of the mid-1970s, the European oil market has been something of a roller-coaster both in terms of price changes, and volumes produced and consumed. The overall effect has been a rise in prices and some decline in volumes.

There were two price peaks in 1974 and again in 1980 related to market pressures brought to bear by the oil-producing countries' cartel, OPEC (Organization of Petroleum Exporting Countries), and by panic buying to secure supplies. There was a third price peak around 1985 due to a sustained currency rise in the US dollar against the ECU (oil is priced in US dollars).

It is no doubt partly for these reasons that it is now European Community (EC) policy to reduce the single market's dependence on oil during the 1990s. By 1988, oil accounted for around 45 per cent of primary energy usage. The stated objective is to reduce this to around 42 per cent by 1995.[1] This has been coupled with moves across Europe to reduce pollution from fuels such as leaded petrol used in transport.[2]

The European oil market for energy is thus unlikely to show major growth over the next ten years.

(Crude oil is also used as a chemical feedstock for the production of organic chemicals. This market tends to be cyclical over several years with a general upward

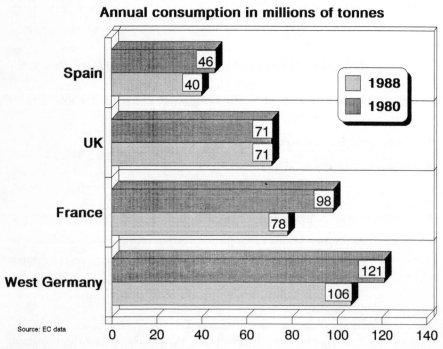

Annual consumption in millions of tonnes

Source: EC data

Figure 3.1   Oil consumption trends in Europe

trend over a longer period. This is expected to continue but oil usage here is much smaller than for primary energy above.)

Within the EC, oil and petrol consumption declined by 120 million tonnes between 1979 and 1985. However, in the years 1986–8, it increased by under 2 per cent per annum, primarily as a result of the transport sector demands.[3] Figure 3.1 summarises consumption for selected countries including the Spanish market.

The major oil companies have been active across Europe for many years. The Seven Sisters (Shell, BP, Exxon, Texaco, Mobil, Chevron and Gulf) are now somewhat depleted following the merger of Chevron-Gulf and the withdrawal of some from some national markets, eg Texaco from Germany, BP from Denmark. The main companies are shown in Table 3.1.

Table 3.1 European oil and petrol companies

		1987 sales US$Mi	Europe total	% sales in home country
Royal Dutch Shell	Neth/UK	65 460	48%	na
British Petroleum	UK	*36 000	72%	40%
ENI	Italy	*15 500	80%	75%
Elf Aquitaine	France	*15 500	87%	80%
Total	France	14 340	na	36%
Petrofina	Belgium	8 650	72%	na
Statoil	Norway	* 8 500	na	na
Neste	Finland	* 4 800	na	na
Veba	Germany	* 4 790	na	na
Repsol	Spain	4 316	95%	85%
Esso Germany only	Germany	4 300	95%	95%
OeMV	Austria	2 086	na	78%
RWE	Germany	1 903	100%	100%
Klockner	Germany	1 438	100%	100%

Note: 1. The above covers petrol and oil sales only and excludes chemicals, mining etc.
2. For turnover shown with *, internal company sales have been estimated and excluded from above.
3. Data for destination of sales are for company overall but the category is such a large part of total turnover that sales % shown above are meaningful.
4. Esso Europe data are not available but the company would be one of the single Europe market leaders.
5. Some other important US companies also do not publish useful European data, eg Mobil, Texaco, Conoco.
6. In 1989, Deutsche Texaco was sold to RWE, Germany for DM2.2bn.

Source: *European Business Strategies*[4]

Crucially company profitability is bound up with upstream and downstream integration: all the major companies above have connections from oil exploration ('upstream') right through to retail sale ('downstream'). With profit margin pressures on refining and retail selling, the upstream parts are important to profit delivery. But downstream is important strategically in providing outlets for an oil company's products.

ENI, Elf, Total, Statoil and Neste are government-owned (or with at least a majority share) companies in their respective countries. They have significant market shares in their home markets. Repsol and OeMV were privatised at least partially by their respective governments in the late 1980s.

Few major strategic moves were reported in the run-up to Europe 1993 to mid-1990: both Texaco and Mobil in Germany have sold out to national companies but this is unlikely to be due to the single market as such, more due to share weakness.

Each of the international oil companies has varying market shares in national countries. There is no one, dominant company across Europe. In some countries, there are strong national brands such as AGIP (ENI) in Italy. Their strength lies not so much in their refining capacity as in their possession of good retail petrol-filling station sites.

With such a fragmented European market, competition is strong and profit margins tend to be low. Periodically, some companies employ either product improvements or promotions to boost sales. But the lack of real product differentiation, as seen by the target group, stops major share building once the good filling sites have been acquired and updated.

Regional national petrol companies are possible and have attained a viable market share in a geographical area: the key again is the well-sited petrol-filling station. In this case, petrol can be bought on the spot market, only adding to the fragmented market share status.

Table 3.2 European retail distribution trends

	Numbers of retail outlets			1988 annual volume per point of retail sale (cubic metres)
	1981	1984	1988	
Germany	24 864	19 288	18 658	2 230
Spain	4 602	4 622	4 821	3 600
France	39 500	36 000	29 000	1 258
UK	24 760	21 705	20 016	1 670

Sources: European Commission and CPDP from *Panorama of EC Industry 1991–92*, Office for Official publications of the EC, pp 1–39.

Table 3.2 shows that there has been some decline in the number of petrol-filling stations over the last ten years. This is partly from a decline in oil consumption and partly for specific national reasons. There is strong competition in Germany and the UK from all the oil majors. In France, major competition has emerged from the supermarket chains which accounted for 31 per cent of all retail petrol sales by 1987: up from 14 per cent in 1983.[5]

As will be seen in Table 3.2, Spain has exceptionally high sales at each petrol station because the number of sites has been strictly controlled as part of a government monopoly. The single market will now allow entry to other companies by 1993.

In addition to retail outlets for petrol, each country has a primary distribution system based on pipeline networks (especially for petrol) and direct tanker deliveries to end-users (especially for diesel fuel). Oil companies share ownership in some of these network systems, which vary according to the country.

SINGLE EUROPE BARRIERS TO TRADE

There have been differences in tax rates, government attitudes to national petrol companies and other issues which have all led to the European structure as we now see it. But overall, the 'single Europe' is less likely to have a major impact than with some other industries because of:

- the global nature of trade;

- freely available supplies;

- international branding of many oil companies;

- strong competition in many markets.

Nevertheless, some significant barriers have been identified by the European Commission. These are reflected in the price comparison for petrol products shown in Table 3.3: over 20 per cent separates the lowest and highest prices.

Table 3.3 Prices for selected oil products in September 1987 (excluding VAT and excise duties)

	Premium petrol	Regular petrol	Residual fuel oil
EC average price for 1000l in ECU	187	164	107
and country variations as % of average			
Germany	92%	90%	92%
Spain	104%	110%	96%
France	95%	114%	93%
UK	106%	114%	112%

Source: European Commission[1]

Table 3.4 summarises the major barriers to the single Europe existing in May 1988, as identified by the European Commission.

Table 3.4 Summary of single Europe barriers in the oil industry

		Countries
1.	Monopoly of exploration	Germany, Italy, Denmark, Ireland, Netherlands
2.	Exploration itemising procedures	All
3.	Controls on oil field development	All
4.	Taxation of oil production	All
5.	Landing obligation for all oil produced in that country	UK, Italy
6.	Restrictions on imports from non-EC countries	France, Portugal, Spain, Germany
7.	Obligation for companies to accept crude oil acquired by State	France, Spain
8.	Obligation to use national flag shipping for carriage	Spain, France, Portugal
9.	Obligation to use national carrier for inland transport	Germany
10.	Exclusive rights to refining (but several companies involved)	Spain, Germany, France, Portugal
11.	Exclusive right to market output of national refineries on the domestic market	Spain
12.	Quantitative restrictions on importation of oil products	Spain, Ireland, Germany, Italy, Portugal
13.	Import licences and declarations for EC oil products	Belgium, Spain, Germany, Portugal
14.	Prohibition of transfrontier deliveries not approved by countries shown right	Spain, Germany, France, Portugal
15.	Differences in rates and technical norms	All
16.	Differences in compulsory storage arrangements	All
17.	Pricing fixing systems	Spain, Greece
18.	Differences in VAT and excise duties	All
19.	Existence of other indirect taxes	Spain, Germany, France, Italy, Portugal.

Source: European Commission[1]

All of these barriers have to be harmonised by 1 January 1993. Some of those involving Spain and Portugal are governed by the gradual move to EC membership and are already agreed. A start has been made on others and many of the restrictions will disappear over the designated period.

The possible implications of the reduction in barriers for the international oil companies are summarised in the BP Annual Report 1987: 'We are . . . thinking hard about our national subsidiaries, recognising that in a more open market it may be possible to eliminate some of the overlap in national functions that it is hard to avoid today.'

For the leading national oil companies like Veba, ENI, Repsol and Elf, the same economies may not be available: they do not have the same extensive trans-European links. However, it is doubtful if this will be crucial to profitability: upstream linkages are being developed inside and outside Europe, and are more important.

THE PROTECTED SPANISH OIL AND PETROL DISTRIBUTION MARKET

In 1987, the Spanish government was considering the liberation of the Spanish oil market which had to be completed by 1992. Essentially up to this time it had been protected behind barriers that had to come down over the period to 1 January 1993:

- any EC company would be able to develop competing retail facilities;

- import restrictions on petroleum products had to be removed by 1992;

- Spain would remove state price-setting and adopt a system of fully negotiable prices set by market conditions.

In 1988, Campsa operated the only integrated network in Spain for the transport, storage and distribution of petroleum products. Specifically, it operated Spain's only pipeline network for oil and petrol distribution: the alternative was tanker haulage. It was owned by the four major Spanish oil distributors: Repsol, Cepsa, Petromed and Ertoil Group, with each having a share according to its share of Spanish refining capacity. Thus Repsol, as the company dominating the Spanish oil market, had 64 per cent of Campsa.

In the liberalisation process, the Spanish government was concerned that too much of the domestic oil market might fall into foreign hands.[6] Thus it wanted Petromed to join together with its bigger domestic rival Cepsa. Shareholdings in both Petromed and Cepsa were dominated by Spanish banks, Banco Central and Banesto respectively.

In addition to its pipeline network, Campsa was the largest owner of Spanish retail petrol outlets. Out of the 4821 retail stations in Spain in 1988, 1800 belonged to Campsa and the rest were linked to the company by long term contracts. Among the remainder were a limited number operated and controlled by Repsol Petroleo.[2]

While no other European oil companies had been able to gain entry into the Spanish market up to 1988, it was well known that the French company, Elf, and the UK company, British Petroleum (BP), had been examining the market. BP had decided that, until the dust settled on the possible implications of Spanish privatisation, it would be difficult to fix its business strategy. But both companies could see real possibilities, depending on what happened at Repsol.

REPSOL SA, SPAIN

Repsol was Spain's largest oil company and it was tenth in Europe. It had grown steadily in turnover and profitability over the years to 1988. As Tables 3.5, 3.6 and 3.7 show, it also had interests in gas distribution and petrochemicals.

Table 3.5 Turnover (pesetas billion)

	1986	1987	1988
Exploration and production	98	105	90
Refining	517	574	590
Distribution of petrol	108	115	126
Petrochemicals	88	97	121
Distribution of LPG*	124	112	112
Intercompany	(102)	(102)	(95)
Total	832	901	942

Table 3.6 Operating income (pesetas billion)

Exploration and production	11	1	10
Refining	16	39	40
Distribution of petrol	12	15	17
Petrochemicals	8	15	31
Distribution of LPG*	5	7	2
Intercompany	1	(2)	–
Total	53	75	99

Table 3.7 Assets (pesetas billion)

	Identifiable assets		Capital expenditures		
	1987	1988	1986	1987	1988
Exploration etc	109	87	17	13	7
Refining	197	174	4	3	9
Distribution	121	132	9	19	31
Petrochemicals	55	65	2	2	6
Distribution LPG*	43	46	4	7	8
Corporate	201	222	–	–	–
Total	725	725	37	43	62

Return on capital 1988: 20.2%
% sales in Europe: over 95
% sales in home country: estimated 85

* LPG means liquid petroleum gas for households.

Repsol Exploracion produced oil in 13 countries. There were two other principal subsidiary companies: Repsol Petroleo and Repsol Butano. Through the latter, the company sold bottled gas and also distributed natural gas to households.

In 1988, Repsol had a dominant position in Spain:

- it distributed 73 per cent of Spanish oil products;

- it had a controlling share in the national oil pipeline chain;

- it distributed practically all the butane *bottled* gas sold in Spain (but only limited involvement in domestic *piped* gas: see below).

Like most oil companies, Repsol had become involved in petrochemicals which it manufactured in Spain. However, its involvement in this sector was subject to all the competitive pressures associated with the large and fragmented European petrochemical market. Thus it was considered that petrochemical sales margins and profitability were at best cyclical, and unlikely to improve dramatically.

Because of its recent privatisation, Repsol's strategies in 1988 were concentrated on consolidation of its new status and also domestic growth. Gas supply was important in this context, as the Spanish market was considered to be in its infancy: it grew +28 per cent 1988 over 1987. The company was examining two major domestic gas suppliers: Gas Madrid, the monopoly supplier of gas to the capital; and Catalana de Gas, the country's biggest distributor with 37 per cent market share. Repsol said that it was aiming for 50 per cent of all the natural gas in the Spanish household/residential sector by 1992.

European expansion was thus not the main focus of its strategy. Nevertheless, in August 1989, Repsol purchased the UK independent companies, Carless Refining and Marketing Ltd and Carless Petroleum Ltd. These companies were involved in the UK in the production, distribution and marketing of petroleum products with 528 service stations.

ELF AQUITAINE SA, FRANCE

Elf Aquitaine is the leading French oil company and fourth in Europe. It is 56 per cent owned by the French government. Its petrol and oil brands, Elf and Antar, are market leaders in France with around 20 per cent of the market. They are followed by the other French petrol company, Total, which is 45 per cent government owned. In 1988, Elf had 5860 filling stations in France compared to 4957 for Total. Elf also had small chains in the UK, The Netherlands, Germany and Belgium, but across all 4 countries these only totalled some 1300 filling stations.

Much of Elf's recent expenditure had been to secure oil supplies and integrate upstream. Thus it acquired the following assets in 1988/9:

- UK North Sea oil gas blocks;

- Dutch North Sea Zone blocks;

- Italian oil rights;

- United States: Michigan and Alaska oil and gas rights;

- 25 per cent of the British independent company, Enterprise Oil.

Elf France sold some 11.5 million tons of oil to the domestic French market in 1988. Outside France, the company sold some 7.2 million tons of oil products in 1988, which represented an increase of 4.2 per cent over 1987. Of these latter sales, 46 per cent were supplied directly by Elf France, either directly or via product swaps or processing agreements; 43 per cent was acquired on the local or international markets and 11 per cent was produced from crude oil refined in outside refineries.

For example, Elf has around 450 sites in the UK with a market share of 2–3 per cent. In January 1990, it purchased another 250 sites from the US oil company Amoco plus refining capacity at Milford Haven, South Wales: it was estimated that this would give Elf another 2 per cent market share. The company said that the purchase was 'necessary to achieve penetration and significant economic advantage.'

Elf was equally interested in expanding into Spain, which it considered an important market for refined products. It had the additional advantage that it was geographically adjacent to southern France. One of its chief strategic tasks was to decide how to achieve this expansion as the Spanish market was opened up.

In the years 1987 and 1988, its revenue had been relatively static as shown in Table 3.8. While profitability had grown over the same time scale as shown in Table 3.9, this was partly due to the cyclical effects of the petrochemical cycle.

Table 3.8 Revenue (francs billion)

	1987	1988
Exploration and production	28.7	28.8
Refining and marketing	38.7	34.1
Chemicals and building materials	30.4	35.1
Health hygiene	12.6	14.6
Holding company and trading	46.0	38.8
Intercompany	(29.0)	(25.4)
Dividends and other income	7.7	8.3
Total	135.1	134.4

Table 3.9 Operating profit after income taxes (francs billion)

	1987	1988
Exploration and production	12.9	12.8
Refining and marketing	–	1.0
Chemicals and building materials	3.6	5.5
Health hygiene	2.2	1.7
Holding company and trading	2.8	5.0
Intercompany	–	–
Total	21.4	25.9

Table 3.10   Assets (francs billion)

| | Assets after depreciation | | Capital expenditure | |
	1987	1988	1987	1988
Exploration etc	46.6	51.8	7.8	7.3
Refining etc	6.0	5.9	1.2	1.0
Chemicals etc	18.7	19.5	1.9	3.1
Health hygiene	3.4	4.8	0.7	2.0
Holding etc	1.5	1.4	0.2	–
Total	76.2	83.4	11.8	13.4

Table 3.11   1988 geographical analysis (francs billion)

	France and trading	Other Europe	Rest of world	Inter-company	Other income
Revenue	101.6	17.8	23.5	(15.3)	8.3
Operating profit after income tax	13.3	6.5	6.1	–	–
Capital expenditure	6.4	2.9	4.1		
Assets after	22.5	29.5	31.4*		

*includes North America: FF15.3bn, Africa: FF15.0bn

Return on capital: 7.4% (before tax)
% sales in Europe: 88
% sales in home country: 77

In 1988, Elf still relied on France to provide most of its sales and profits, as shown in Table 3.11.

BRITISH PETROLEUM, UK

British Petroleum was the second largest oil and petroleum company in Europe. In terms of numbers of filling stations in 1988, it was ranked in the first five in the UK, Netherlands, Greece, Ireland, France, Portugal, Luxembourg, Germany and Belgium. It also had substantial sales and resources in the US.

Tables 3.12, 3.13 and 3.14 show that both turnover and operating profits derived from a broad spread of interests with the USA being a leading contributor.

Table 3.12 Turnover (£m)

	1987	1988
UK	11 454	10 551
Rest of Europe	8 163	7 326
USA	9 458	8 421
Rest of world	3 507	2 931
less intergroup	(4 254)	(3 307)
Total	28 328	25 922
Exploration and production	6 452	5 833
Refining and manufacturing	20 104	16 767
Chemicals	2 760	3 254
Minerals	446	738
Nutrition	1 843	1 973
Coal	627	539
Other	430	152
less intergroup	(4 334)	(3 329)
Total	28 328	25 922

Table 3.13 Operating profits before tax (£m)

	1987	1988
UK	751	828
Rest of Europe	319	394
USA	1 478	1 303
Rest of world	263	366
Total	2 811	2 891

Table 3.14 Assets (£m)

	1987	1988
UK	2 625	5 374
Rest of Europe	2 526	2 327
USA	9 432	9 210
Rest of world	2 658	3 278
Total	17 241	20 189

BP was now considering its options for entering the Spanish oil and petrol market. Along with other European leaders such as Esso and Texaco, it was examining possible entry options.

Table 3.15 US$ exchange rates (June averages)

	1987	1988
French franc	6.0728	5.9294
German mark	1.8186	1.7571
Spanish peseta	126.261	116.2091
UK£	0.6139	0.563

CASE QUESTIONS

1. How can Repsol defend its dominant share of the Spanish oil and petrol market as the single Europe barriers come down?

2. How can other companies, such as Elf and BP, attack this market? What strategies will be most cost effective in the long term?

REFERENCES

1. European Commission, COM (88) 238, 'Internal Energy Market', Office for official publications of the EC, Luxembourg.
2. *Panorama of EC Industry 1990*, p 1–10, Office for the official publications of the EC, Luxembourg.
3. Ibid, p 1–31.
4. Lynch, R (1990) *European Business Strategies*, Kogan Page, London.
5. *Panorama of EC Industry 1989*, p 1–28.
6. *Financial Times*, 6 June 1991, p 15.

4

BAT Tobacco moves into Eastern Europe*

Referring to the political and economic changes taking place in Eastern Europe, the chairman of BAT Industries (UK), Sir Patrick Sheehy, described the beginning of the 1990s as the most exciting era he had seen in 40 years in the tobacco industry.[1]

In 1990, BAT Industries plc, one of the world's largest tobacco companies, had become increasingly optimistic about the market opportunities opening up in Eastern Europe. World market volume sales in 1989 were around 5300 billion cigarettes per annum with +1 per cent annual growth. For political reasons, two-thirds of this world market had been closed to Western tobacco companies because it was behind the Iron and Bamboo Curtains of Eastern Europe and China.

As a result of the changes that have taken place, Eastern European markets then opened up. Initially, BAT exported cigarettes from the West. But it was the company's view that the real opportunities were to be gained by manufacturing and marketing in Eastern Europe.

The main issues were as follows.

- What was the size of the opportunity?

- What were the risks? Were they worth the business exposure?

- How could the risks be minimised?

- What was the optimal entry method? Joint venture? Takeover? Continued exports?

This case explores the evidence.

EUROPEAN CIGARETTE MARKETS

In spite of extensive publicity about the dangers of smoking tobacco and cigarettes, European Community (EC) consumption of cigarettes per head of the population declined by only 2 per cent in total between 1980 and 1988.[2] Even in 1988, consumption per head across the EC averaged 1764 cigarettes per annum.

---

*This case has been prepared from published data sources only. © Copyright Aldersgate Consultancy Limited 1993.

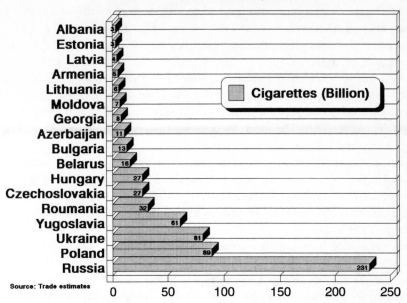

Figure 4.1 Cigarette consumption in Eastern Europe

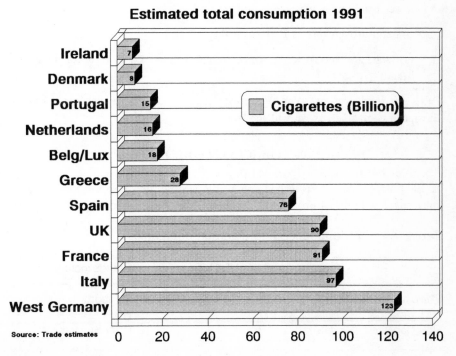

Figure 4.2 Cigarette consumption in the EC

Reliable historical data on Eastern European consumption are not available, because the former communist countries had no interest in measuring and meeting customer demand. However, data for 1991 are available: see Figures 4.1 and 4.2.

Importantly for assessing marketing potential, the Western emphasis on the health hazards of cigarettes was not shared by Eastern European countries. For example, smoking was seen as socially acceptable in a harsh economic climate in Russia.[3] Before Yugoslavia was ripped apart by war, I personally observed the same phenomenon among young senior management executives attending a seminar in Serbia in September 1991. The main difficulty for smokers in Eastern Europe was that demand perpetually outstripped supply.

Moreover, cigarettes were often bartered like currency: I also observed cigarettes being used to pay for a car parking place in Budapest in September 1992. For similar reasons, cigarette smuggling had become an organised crime in Poland in 1992.[4] This all made cigarette marketing in Eastern Europe very different from cigarette marketing in the West.

Given the choice between Western and Eastern cigarette brands, some early market research evidence suggested that customers preferred Western products: real data are sketchy but an East German survey by the market research company A C Nielsen in 1992 supported this view.[5] Better packaging and better quality tobacco and manufacturing probably all contributed to this impression. However, by 1993, there was some evidence[5] of a switch back to Eastern European brands because of:

- lower prices than Western products;

- some improvements in Eastern quality;

- nostalgia and special tastes which were better served by traditional national brands.

Partly for these reasons, some Western tobacco companies have acquired Eastern European companies, as we will see later.

BAT TOBACCO WORLDWIDE

In 1990, BAT Tobacco was second only to the US company, Philip Morris, in global tobacco sales. Table 4.1 provides the evidence. The American company leads partly

Table 4.1 World tobacco and cigarette companies

		Sales US$ billion	Brands include
Philip Morris	US	21	Marlboro
BAT Tobacco	UK	17	HB
RJR Nabisco	US	8	Peter Stuyvesant

Source: Company accounts

as a result of its 43 per cent share of the large American market. By contrast, BAT is more international in its source of sales.

In 1991, BAT Tobacco was particularly strong in Europe in terms of sales, but its major source of profits was North America, where cigarette profit margins for all brands were higher than elsewhere in the world. Table 4.2 shows the background information.

Table 4.2 BAT Tobacco worldwide activity

Year ended 31st December 1991			US$ millions
	Turnover	*Profit**	*Assets***
UK	552	112	440
Rest of Europe	4 643	197	688
North America	3 316	813	1 173
Australasia	971	24	267
Latin America	3 412	240	476
Asia	1 425	173	343
Africa	587	76	176
Total	14 906	1 635	3 563

*Profit: before tax and interest
**Total assets less non-operating assets and operating creditors.

Note: 1. In addition, BAT had US$8804 million turnover in financial services. This area of the company's business was managed totally seperately by the company and is therefore not included in the above.
2. BAT Tobacco also had a series of associated tobacco companies around the world that were not consolidated into the above accounts: turnover was US$4595 million. (Table 4.1 includes this additional turnover).

Source: company accounts converted at US$/£1.7256

While it could be argued that the USA and Canada should have received first consideration for further BAT Tobacco investment, BAT Tobacco was aware of its vulnerable US strategic position: its share of the US market was one quarter the size of the market leader (11 per cent versus 43 per cent). This view was justified by subsequent events. In early 1993, the market leader, Philip Morris, cut the prices of its leading brands by around 20 per cent in North America with BAT being forced to follow,[6] thus reducing profit margins.

BAT TOBACCO AND EASTERN EUROPE

By 1991, BAT Tobacco had made a number of significant moves into Eastern Europe. The company regarded these areas as holding great potential for the future: its tobacco growing and manufacturing expertise, coupled with its skills at marketing and branding, contrasted strongly with the current activities and products from the former Communist State factories on sale at that time.

BAT exports from western Europe

BAT's German company had factories in Bayreuth (in Bavaria) and Berlin. In 1990, it exported 1 billion cigarettes mainly under its HB brand to Hungary, the Czech and Slovak Republics, the republics of the former states of Yugoslavia and the USSR. Difficulties that have been encountered with exports to Eastern Europe include:

- need for payment in hard currency or the arrangement of barter deals (which take time and cost part of the profit margin);

- higher prices for imported cigarettes as a result of tariffs (up to 30 per cent premium in some cases);

- little control over distribution and sale;

- lack of a permanent presence in the country to build a brand and long-term franchise.

BAT joint venture in Hungary

In early 1991, BAT negotiated a joint venture with the State-owned factory at Pecsi, Hungary. The local company already supplied 40 per cent of the national market from a factory employing 800 people. The Hungarian cigarette market size was 27 billion cigarettes per annum in 1991.[1] To win the contract, BAT had to beat strong counter-bids from other companies including Japan Tobacco, Reetsma and Rothmans.

BAT was attracted to the deal because it offered a major move into a market with a company having significant market share. The Hungarian State company benefited from BAT's injection of US$34 million into its operations: it was to be used for plant modernisation, higher quality products, and building a more efficient sales and distribution network. In addition, BAT was willing to assist the Hungarian company improve the quality and yield of its locally grown tobacco crop through technical help.

In the first year, BAT and the Hungarian joint venture made great efforts to improve the distribution of existing products. One of the real problems with the previous command economy had been that products were only available when the factory decided to supply them. Systems and management attitudes were revised to ensure that the basic product range was consistently in distribution. Promotional incentives to develop distribution and shop display, both among the joint venture's distributors and among participating retailers, were also examined. Technical systems were also introduced to monitor and assist the consistent distribution of the product range.

Pricing was another area that had to be tackled, but with annual inflation at +35 per cent in Hungary during 1991,[7] it was difficult to make any real impact. Until consistent distribution was secured, advertising support was considered less important. However, the company judged that it was vital to identify the leading brand and support distribution of this product.

The first year proved rewarding for the joint venture with a claimed increase in brand share from 40 to 50 per cent and a strengthening of its leading brand, Sobranie. Results were achieved not only by technology improvements but also by better use of the skilled workforce.

Difficulties encountered included the following:[3]

- Management problems arising from the need to make a profit. The company had a history and tradition of making losses, since these had previously been covered by an automatic State subsidy.

- The workforce was used to being remunerated by being given holiday homes and free accommodation rather than being paid higher wages.

- The retail trade and distribution network was suprised. After years of selling what the State monopoly decided to send, it was a major change to find that the sales orders requested were the actual orders delivered.

More generally, BAT Tobacco commented that they still regarded the Hungarian venture as being long term in nature with little real profit inside ten years.

BAT bids for business in Czechoslovakia and Poland

In 1992, BAT Tobacco was also invited to bid for the Czechoslovak tobacco group, Tabak. The State company produced 20 billion cigarettes annually and had around 70 per cent of market.[8] Its 1991 sales were Kcs 4 billion (US$ 133 million). A separate Slovakian company supplied the rest of the market.

BAT's bid was unsuccessful with Philip Morris (US) gaining the contract: the US company had pledged around US$400 million in cash and capital expenditure.[9] BAT later complained that the Czechoslovak State authorities had already concluded that the US company would gain the deal and only invited BAT into the bidding process to make the list appear more open.[3] Clearly the attraction of the deal for the winner lay, partially at least, in acquiring a dominant market share.

In Poland, BAT Tobacco was invited to bid for one or more of the regional cigarette companies. However, the Polish government's policy appeared to be privatise the market on a piecemeal basis. This meant that significant market share could not be purchased and it made the idea less attractive.[3]

Developments in the former USSR

In 1991 and 1992, BAT Tobacco began the process of examining the countries that made up the former Soviet Union. Its senior managers visited over half the 26 factories existing in the USSR. Their initial conclusions were that the tobacco markets in some republics were attractive.

In spite of the political uncertainties that increased the investment risk, the company decided to proceed. In November 1992 BAT opened formal negotiations for a joint venture in the Russian Republic with Moscow's largest cigarette factory.

'Formal negotiations' meant that the company started talking with the factory's 1400 workers, as central government decision making needed to be complemented by local discussions. In addition, BAT also started talks with the city, regional government and regulatory authorities on the shape of the venture. The whole process would need patience and time.

In early 1993 BAT started discussions on two more joint ventures in the Ukraine at:

- Prilucky, where BAT established that the factory also supported a sports stadium and two schools.

- Cherkassy, where BAT were also offering to help the company improve its tobacco crop and leaf production yields.

BAT Tobacco also announced around this time that it was examining two more factories in the Russian Republic, one in Moscow and another in Siberia further east.

CASE QUESTIONS

1. What difficulties should BAT look out for in conducting the negotiations in Russia and the Ukraine? How might it overcome these problems? What advice would you offer BAT on the risks involved?

2. Are there any useful lessons on market entry to be drawn from its Czech, Hungarian and Polish exeriences that could be applied to the former USSR?

3. What considerations should the company adopt in its approach to marketing and advertising brands in Russia and the Ukraine? Should it introduce international brands or concentrate on those already available in the country?

REFERENCES

1. Rawsthorne P (1991) 'Tobacco giant taps into new political order', *Financial Times*, 21 January.
2. European Commission, *Panorama of EC Industry 1991/92*, p 102, table 6.
3. Rawsthorne, P (1992) 'BAT poised to light up new market' *Financial Times*, 4 November, p 28.

4. de Jonquieres, G (1992) 'From bare shelves to blue jeans', *Financial Times*, 10 June, p 18.
5. Browning, E J (1993) 'Consumers in parts of Eastern Europe begin to shift back to local products as the lure of forbidden fruit fades', *Wall Street Journal Europe*, 20 January, p 4.
6. Tait, N (1993) 'Marlboro cowboy wants more territory', *Financial Times*, 5 April, p 17.
7. OECD (1992) 'Economic outlook number 52', December, p 123.
8. Genillard, A (1992) 'Czech tobacco group draws bids', *Financial Times*, 9 April, p 30.
9. Genillard, A (1992) 'Philip Morris Czech deal approved', *Financial Times*, 24 April, p 26.

5

Philips Whirlpool and the pan-European customer*

Whirlpool is the US market leader in domestic appliances, such as refrigerators and washing machines. In January 1989, it paid the European electronics group Philips $US470 million for a 53 per cent stake in the European company's domestic appliance subsidiary.[1] Combined with its leadership in the US, this gave Whirlpool global market leadership in domestic appliances.

The problem for Whirlpool was that many European consumers had never heard of its brand name. It was even difficult to pronounce in some languages. Moreover, while it was agreed with Philips that the latter company's well-known brand name could continue on domestic appliances in Europe, the agreement would run for only ten years. Thus, by 1998 at the latest, Whirlpool had to have established itself as a pan-European brand from scratch.

This case examines the process that Whirlpool used to develop its pan-European branding and company presentation. It raises a number of marketing issues, the most important being the identification of the pan-European customer, if such a creature exists!

EUROPEAN MARKET FOR DOMESTIC APPLIANCES

In 1989, the European Community (EC) market for domestic appliances was estimated to be worth around US$20bn and growing at significantly over 5 per cent per annum. All such estimates are approximate because of the difficulty of currency conversion for those European currencies outside the exchange rate mechanism (ERM) and because of the variable parity rates between the ERM and the US$. Sales by the leading EC countries are shown in Figure 5.1.

Included in the domestic appliance market definition are washing machines, fridges and freezers, electric cookers, vacuum cleaners and microwave cookers. There were very large differences in growth rates between the various EC countries, depending principally on changes in the wealth of the population, the differences in climate and cooking tastes. For example, markets in countries like Germany and France were estimated to be growing around 10 per cent per annum.

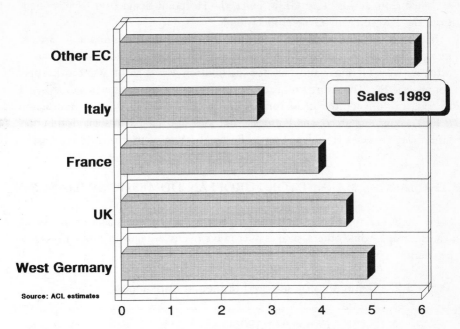

Figure 5.1 Estimated sales of domestic appliances

DOMESTIC APPLIANCE MANUFACTURERS

While domestic appliance manufacture is a worldwide business, many items are made in the geographical region of sale. They are considered to be too heavy and bulky for their value added to be shipped economically around the globe. [Microwave ovens are the main exception: Japanese manufacturers were the main suppliers in this area.] Hence the decision of Whirlpool to acquire a company in Europe. Table 5.1 shows some of the world's largest manufacturers but there are also many smaller producers.

Table 5.1 Leading companies' worldwide sales of domestic appliances

		US$ million 1987	1988
Whirlpool	US	4 200	8 200
General electric	US	4 350	5 900
Electrolux	Sweden	5 100	5 300
Matsushita	Japan	4 180	4 180
Bosch Siemens	Germany	2 200	2 500
Philips	Netherlands	2 000	–

Source: company accounts

The large increases in sales 1987/8 for Whirlpool and General Electric (GE) stemmed from acquisitions: GE included the Hotpoint brand from 1988, bought from the UK company General Electric plc.

In the case of Whirlpool, there were thus two distinct sources of sales: USA and Europe. In Europe, almost all of the Philips Whirlpool products were manufactured in West Germany and Italy for distribution across all of Western Europe, not just the EC. They were thus subject to currency fluctuations, when distributed to countries outside the ERM (principally the European Free Trade Association (EFTA) countries, Greece and Portugal), and were also subject to some distribution inflexibility as they were shipped across Europe because of the distances involved.

THE TARGET MARKET FOR EUROPEAN DOMESTIC APPLIANCES

Some domestic appliances, such as refrigerators, are in the majority of homes across Europe, while others, such as microwave ovens, are only in a minority. Data by country are shown in Table 5.2.

Table 5.2   Ownership of selected domestic appliances

| | (% homes in 1986) | | | |
	Vacuum cleaner	Refrigerator	Microwave oven	Washing machine
Belgium	92	93	7	85
Denmark	72	83	5	60
France	88	96	7	83
Greece	37	72	–	40
Ireland	71	92	8	76
Italy	79	86	9	91
Netherlands	98	97	12	85
Portugal	45	72	–	30
Spain	44	92	–	92
UK	96	91	25	81
West Germany	97	90	18	75

Source: European Commission and ACL estimates

The European domestic appliances market could be regarded as being divided between two types: replacement demand and innovative demand. For products such as vacuum cleaners, many households already had the product. There was little real technological innovation so growth in such markets relied on replacement demand.

For other products that were still to be introduced into many European households, such as microwave ovens and dishwashers, it was considered that real growth potential existed as standards of living improved, thus giving rise to innovative demand. The higher growth rates quoted above for the domestic appliance industry were considered to be largely in this sector.

Within any product category, most target customers were reported to see each manufacturer's products as being similar. There was not much difference in intrinsic quality and performance.

The prime target group was regarded as being women. They were probably married with a family. While they certainly cared about their families, they also led an active life beyond the confines of household and valued the use of labour-saving devices such as domestic appliances.

THE NEW PHILIPS WHIRLPOOL MARKETING MIX

As announced in March 1990,[2] there were three main elements to the new marketing strategy for Philips Whirlpool domestic appliances:

1. pan-European advertising and branding;

2. new top quality service arrangements;

3. special retail financial packages.

In addition, Philips Whirlpool would be competitive on price bands within the product categories it was selling. But it would major on the areas above.

Advertising is covered in more detail later: this would be standardised across Europe. The other two strategies were also regarded as being highly important but would be subject to local, ie national country, variation and final decision. These are described next.

Marketing mix: service arrangements

Coinciding with the pan-European advertising campaign, the company introduced a service package which the company claimed would be as good as any in the industry. First, the company's guarantee would be honoured anywhere in the EC.

Within this overall warranty, the company provided a further level of service that varied with each country. For example, in the UK it offered to replace any machine that could not be repaired during the first year of purchase or refund the full purchase price. All parts were guaranteed for ten years for a single payment of £12.50 (US$22.30). A customer telephone hot line was installed at Whirlpool's UK headquarters to provide centralised customer service. Customer service engineers were retrained and reorganised, and spare part availability was also revamped.

Marketing mix: retail financial packages

To obtain good in-store display, the company was offering the retailer special financial packages to cover not only display stock in the retail area, but, in some cases, the store's whole inventory of Philips Whirlpool products.

Because of variation in distribution patterns between countries, the detail behind the general principle was subject to local variation.

PHILIPS WHIRLPOOL PAN-EUROPEAN ADVERTISING

As a matter of principle, the new company decided to retain in the early years the dual branding identity by using both Philips and Whirlpool names.[2, 3]

Jan Karel, managing director and chief operating officer of Whirlpool International, was reported as explaining that, by putting the two names together, you get the best of both. They reinforce each other with the positive, established feelings associated with Philips combining with the new associations of the Whirlpool name. In summary, Whirlpool's innovation added to Philips' knowledge and background.

In practice, the research evidence from a survey of 1080 European women did not entirely agree. They did not have the same clear view of the Whirlpool brand name. The advertising had to go through several phases for the final work to emerge:[2]

Phase 1: Basic survey of 1080 members of the target group in 4 European countries.

Phase 2: Interviews on two outline advertising campaigns based on the earlier findings.

Phase 3: Final advertising based on the evidence of the responses to the Phase 2 material.

Specifically, the advertising development was managed by the Philips company. It relied on fully tested and researched campaigns rather than creative judgement. This meant that research evidence was paramount and the phases above took around one year to bring to fruition.

Phase 1: initial survey

This was conducted by the French research agency, TMO, and interviewed 1080 women in the target group in four countries, Austria, the UK, Spain and France. Each was researched individually in an interview lasting around one hour.

The results showed that the target group aspired to the status of leading a modern active life, even if, in all cases, this was not necessarily the current situation. However, more detailed research of the name Whirlpool brought some complications: it was unpronounceable in some languages, 'W' does not exist in the Spanish language and is difficult in French. Nevertheless, it was decided to retain the name because it gave a new and exciting image to the brand, and was not as potentially condescending as the Latinisation of an Anglo-Saxon brand name.

The research also showed that housewives were unimpressed by the size of the Whirlpool company. One respondent noted that size could be achieved by acquisition and would do nothing for product quality in itself.

The target group in the UK and Austria also produced some adverse reaction to open American associations. German products were seen as being more likely to be innovative, while US products were associated more with a fast-food, disposable society that lacked discrimination. The agency concluded that this meant that a creative theme introducing the new modern world from the USA was unlikely to be successful. The US associations were therefore not developed in the advertising campaign that followed.

Phase 2: advertising development

Advertising development was co-ordinated by the Philips Whirlpool French-based advertising agency, Publicis FCS International. The agency works on a federal structure across Europe with offices in major European capitals. For this campaign, there was a lead agency office which then sent creative development briefs to four Publicis agencies in London, Milan, Paris and Barcelona.

The outline advertising brief said that it was necessary to make it clear that Whirlpool and its logo were a company, not just a new name from Philips. It also had to highlight Philips and its logo very clearly, and explain that it had come together with Whirlpool. Both companies would need to be mentioned several times in the campaign. More generally, to be successful as pan-European advertising, the advertising brief indicated that the creative treatment needed to find the common ground in the target group that would overcome national preferences.

Five initial campaign ideas were developed by the four advertising offices. Using further research interviews, these were then reduced to two more detailed commercials: 'The Machines that Make Things Good' from Paris and 'Beautiful to Live With' from London. The Paris treatment followed a strong creative treatment with a popular French tune, 'I am a Gigolo' and liberated, young, modern adults. The London advertising was more emotional and oriented towards the home.

Both campaigns were then subjected to further testing in France, the UK and Austria. The results showed that neither was entirely successful. The French target group liked the French campaign and rejected the more homely, emotional British commercial. The UK preferred the more home-oriented campaign and did not like the modern French campaign. The Austrians rejected them both, principally because they were associated with America, though this had not been mentioned in the test commercial.

Phase 3: final advertising

One possible conclusion from the research was to run two campaigns, one in southern Europe, based on the Paris work and one in northern Europe, based on the London work. However, the research agency pointed out that a campaign idea that had been rejected in the early days because it was too bland had actually researched well everywhere.

This was an information campaign explaining the benefits of the new combination of Philips and Whirlpool. It was called 'Brings Quality to Life' and was developed and researched again. This time the advertising researched well in all countries. The result was something of a suprise to all those involved, but it was decided to adopt the campaign.

The final commercial was broadcast across 14 European countries in spring 1990. The opening campaign expenditure was set at around $US50 million with around 20 per cent being allocated to the UK.

Over several years, it was planned to spend around US$110 million on the advertising campaign to establish the Whirlpool name.[3] By 1998, the Philips name would have to be dropped, but this would only be done when the local company judged that the local market was ready.

CASE QUESTIONS

1. What are the benefits of pan-European branding? What resources are required to generate such benefits?
2. What are the strengths and weaknesses of the approach adopted in 1990 by Whirlpool?
3. Is pan-European branding the best solution to the marketing opportunity facing Whirlpool?
4. Where does pan-European activity stop and national activity take over?
5. Does the pan-European customer exist in domestic appliances?

REFERENCES

1. Tait, N and van de Krol, R (1991) 'The final link in Whirlpool's global circle', *Financial Times*, 7 June, p 15.
2. Harris, C (1990) 'Women of Europe put Whirlpool in a spin', *Financial Times*, 1 March, p 24.
3. *The Economist* (1991) 'But will it wash?', 13 July, p 84.

6

Marketing research for Courtaulds' new 'Tencel' fibre*

In early 1993, the UK international textile company Courtaulds plc officially launched a revolutionary new textile fibre called 'Tencel'. The event was the culmination of 14 years of development at a cost of £45 million, with another £55 million being spent on a production plant at Mobile, Alabama, USA.

An important marketing issue facing the company at this time was how to launch the product across Europe. The marketing research evidence about the fibre's European prospects was limited: the data needed to guide the decision are the subject of this case.

EUROPEAN TEXTILE AND CHEMICAL FIBRE MARKETS

In examining the marketing issues, it is useful to split the background factors surrounding the new product into two subsectors: the European market for chemical fibres and the European textile market. In practice, there is considerable interaction between them, because fibres are used to make textile yarns, fabrics and clothing. Courtaulds operates in both market areas.

European market for chemical fibres

This market consists solely of the manufacture and sale of chemical fibres, such as nylon, some of which are made into yarn. All the fibres are produced in large, specially designed plant. The industry is dominated by major European chemical fibre companies such as Hoechst (Germany), ICI (UK) and Du Pont (USA). They operate with significant economies of scale and have strong technical barriers to market entry. After manufacture, the fibres are then used in many of the textile industries outlined in the section below.

While European companies are large, Western Europe production of 3.5 million

---

*This case has been prepared from published data sources only. © Copyright Aldersgate Consultancy Limited 1993.

tonnes in 1989 was only 18 per cent of the world total: the newly independent countries (NICs) made over 50 per cent of global production.[1] During the early 1990s, there was actually excess production capacity in the EC[2] with the European Commission placing increased import duties on fibres from the NICs to protect Europe.

In terms of marketing strategy, European companies in the EC have been moving to higher added-value speciality fibres, where the competition was less fierce and profit margins were therefore higher. Their strategy was, at least partially, to leave cheap, bulk fibre manufacture to the NICs. Courtauld's new 'Tencel' fibre fell firmly into the speciality category.

European textile market

This market covers the manufacture and finishing of yarns, and the production of clothing. It includes all industrial and domestic textiles, and their production into clothing, including fashion items. Over the years 1960–90, new chemical fibres with unusual properties, such as exceptional stretching or durability, had been introduced to this market by the large European fibre producers above: this had provided some real innovation.

European Community textiles production amounted to over US$118 billion in 1990 with the sector employing over 1.5 million workers.[3] The EC was the world's largest exporter and importer of textile products: exports totalled US$15.55 billion and imports US$13.86 billion in 1990.[4] In addition, there was strong trade across the Community.

Against this background, parts of the industry were highly fragmented with many small and medium-sized companies, especially in Greece, Portugal and Italy. Typically, they were involved in assembling and finishing clothing with many firms having less than 20 employees.[3] Barriers to market entry were low and there were few technical economies of scale.

The main marketing strategies for larger companies were to seek higher added value through branding, fashion markets and quality products, and avoid competing directly with the smaller firms. As one of the larger companies, Courtaulds followed these policies.

COURTAULDS' TEXTILE ACTIVITIES

With 1991 sales of UK£922 million (US$1591 million), Courtaulds had a long history of involvement in European and world textile markets. It was involved in both of the areas described above. However, by 1991, it had much larger sales in the branded fabric and clothing end of the market compared with its turnover in basic fibre production, as can be seen in Figure 6.1.

Because it was loss making, Courtaulds slimmed down its spinning operations during 1990/1 and withdrew from areas where it was strategically weak. It was in this poor profit context that the company sought chemical fibres and yarns for

Annual sales 1991 £ Million

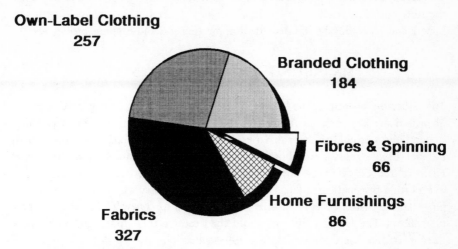

Own-Label Clothing
257

Branded Clothing
184

Fibres & Spinning
66

Home Furnishings
86

Fabrics
327

Note: intra-group sales eliminated
from above data

Source: Company accounts

Figure 6.1   Courtaulds Textiles plc

specialist uses, and products with greater complexity and added value. One such product was its new fibre 'Tencel'.

COURTAULDS' NEW 'TENCEL'

When introduced in 1992, Courtaulds' new Tencel fibre had special properties that gave unique characteristics to finished textiles: garments had the appearance of rough denim but were soft when touched. The overall effect was closer to silk in terms of the way the fabric draped but velvet in terms of the way it felt.

In addition to its luxury appearance when made up into fabric, Courtaulds discovered that its new fibre also had other advantages: it had double the strength of cotton in its dry state and was even stronger wet. Hence it was possible for textile manufacturers such as dyers, finishers, weavers and knitters who sometimes employ a wet manufacturing process, to make a wide range of new products that would compete strongly for a segment of the cotton market. Since cotton accounted for roughly one-third of the world's consumption of fibres by weight,[5] it was judged that Tencel had real sales potential.

Moreover, Tencel's strength when wet meant that its performance was superior to another artificial fibre, Rayon, which had been marketed as long ago as the

1920s and accounted for roughly another 20 per cent of world consumption. In addition, although Tencel was made from similar raw materials to Rayon, its production process was more environmentally friendly than that of Rayon.

Overall, Courtaulds pereived no direct competition for Tencel. They expected the fibre to act by itself or in combination with other fibres to provide stronger, lighter and more durable cloths with unique textural and draping properties.

MARKETING STRATEGY FOR TENCEL

To market the new fibre, the Tencel international marketing manager, Alan Jones, identified his key early customers in 1992 as being fashion leaders in clothing design houses around the world. To keep the early product exclusive, only a small number of designers were allocated cloth: the UK's Zandra Rhodes and Anne Klein of the US were among the famous names who produced clothing using Tencel for a test market in Japan in late 1992: the country was selected because its high-earning customers could afford to pay US$300 for a new Tencel jacket or pair of trousers. The US and Europe would then receive their first taste of the new fibre in the fashion designers' spring 1993 collections.

The marketing manager explained that fabric makers and clothing designers were effectively part of Courtaulds' sales drive, not just its customers. They were a method of demonstrating just what the new fibre could do for other potential customers in exciting and interesting ways.

Not all industry commentators judged Courtaulds' marketing strategy to be the most profitable. They pointed out that when the major UK chemical fibre company ICI plc had launched its new nylon fibre, Tactel, in 1983, it had adopted a different strategy. ICI identified a single specialist market where the product's characteristics would be uniquely successful: the sportswear market. The company then concentrated on this for five years.

It was not until 1989 that ICI launched Tactel to the fashion trade: by this time, its special properties were well understood and it had been positioned as a unique, upmarket fibre. To underline the point, ICI watchers pointed out that by 1991 Tactel had become so successful that it accounted for 35 per cent of ICI's total fibre revenue by value:[6] a remarkable new product statistic for any company.

In addition, ICI was only one of a number of European chemical fibre producers and was not the largest. There were also US producers with unique fibres, eg Du Pont (US) had successfully introduced 'Lycra' stretch yarns into Europe.

TENCEL'S CUSTOMERS

One of the marketing problems facing Du Pont, ICI and Courtaulds was that, outside a few leading clothing manufacturers such as Adidas (Germany) and Levi Jeans (US) and a few major retailers such as Marks & Spencer (UK) and Bennetton (Italy), many of the fibre industry's potential customers were very fragmented. They were small manufacturers who competed using the low labour costs of southern and Eastern Europe, the Far East and elsewhere. This made it more difficult for companies such as Courtaulds to devise a European customer marketing strategy for new fibres such as Tencel.

CASE QUESTIONS

1. What commercially available desk research material is available that would provide further evidence useful to the development of Tencel's European marketing strategy?

2. Is there a case for interviewing potential customers in different European countries? What are the problems with this approach?

3. What further marketing research would you recommend is undertaken to establish European marketing strategy?

REFERENCES

1. European Commission (1991) *Panorama of EC Industry 1991/92*, OPOCE, Luxembourg, p 8–67.
2. Abrahams, P (1992) 'Du Pont faces tough test of fibre', *Financial Times*, 4 November, p 33.
3. European Commission (1991) *Panorama of EC Industry 1991/92*, OPOCE, Luxembourg, p 16–2.
4. Williams, F (1992) 'Many textile quota curbs may linger on', *Financial Times*, 21 February, p 3.
5. Eurostat (1991) *Basic statistics of the Community*, 28th edn, OPOCE, Luxembourg, pp 171 and 172.
6. Green, D. (1993) 'Dethroning King Cotton', *Financial Times*, 5 January, p 11.

7

Strategy options for Irish telephones*

You are a consultant advising an Irish electrical goods company with the following profile.

- It makes electronic telephones. It manufactures the plastic case, buys some of the inside electronics and assembles the complete handset. There are various models in the current range and the company has the ability to add to these. Ex-factory prices range from the equivalent of £UK5 to £UK25 each (£UK1 = US$1.70].

- The telephones are currently sold in very small quantities to the European Community (EC) for household and office use.

- The company's objectives are to earn 60 per cent of its revenue from other members of the EC within five years and to maintain its current current profitability of 15 per cent return on capital before tax. Its total turnover is growing steadily at 14 per cent per annum and is the equivalent of UK£5 million in the current year.

- Exporting to other members of the EC the company's products will compete internationally with those from inside the EC, plus others from Sweden, Singapore, Hong Kong, Korea and Taiwan.

- Currently, the company has a viable share of the telephone handset market in the UK through office equipment companies. The UK accounts for 30 per cent of total turnover.

THE MARKET FOR TELEPHONE HANDSETS IN THE EC

It was estimated by the European Commission[1] that the EC market for telephone handsets was worth around US$1.6 billion in 1987. Trade flows into and out of the EC were very high in this market with very limited barriers to entry across much of Europe. The EC market was growing at around 7 per cent pa.

As background, the EC had one of the largest telephone networks in the world

---

*This case was prepared from published data and private survey information on a company whose identity has been disguised. © Copyright Aldersgate Consultancy Ltd, 1993.

with 123 million lines in 1987, an average of about 38 main lines per 100 inhabitants. By comparison, the USA had 126 million lines (52 per 100 inhabitants) and Japan 49 million (38 per 100 inhabitants).

Within the overall EC figures, there were considerable differences between member states.

Table 7.1 EC subscriber lines 1987

	Number (millions)	per 100 inhabitants
West Germany	27.5	45.6
France	24.8	44.6
United Kingdom	22.9	40.8
Italy	19.0	33.3
Spain	10.2	26.2
Netherlands	6.2	42.7
Greece	3.5	35.0
Belgium	3.4	34.5
Denmark	2.6	52.0
Portugal	1.6	15.8
Ireland	0.8	22.3
Luxembourg	0.2	45.9

Source: European Commission[1]

Almost half of the EC total telecommunications equipment market of US$26 billion in 1987 consisted of public network equipment: all the main telephone service providers were publicly owned except in the UK. Nevertheless, companies and private customers were also substantial purchasers of telephone equipment. Specifically, there was a vigorous private market in telephone handsets in most EC countries.

Within Europe, the main area of technical advance over the next ten years was expected to be the continued investment in the digitisation of the networks. This would allow greatly enhanced telecommunications services such as cheaper electronic data interchange and video telephones.[2]

EC TELEPHONE HANDSETS MARKET – NOTE ON COMPETITIVE ACTIVITY AND MARKET OPPORTUNITIES

Across the EC, the market for telephone handsets was highly fragmented with no dominant suppliers. Because of the relatively simple technology and low added value, manufacturers found it difficult to produce sustainable competitive advantage. It was useful to divide the market into two segments across the EC: the domestic market and the office market.

The domestic market

This was the market for the purchase of individual telephone handsets. The majority of telephones were standard and sold at prices equivalent to the range US$20–40 (UK£12–25). They were sold through electrical retailers and department stores in some countries, eg the UK. In other countries where the government still controlled the telecommunications industry, such as Italy, they were sold through the national telecommunications service company. Distribution was vital to attacking this market which sold largely on price.

Within the domestic market, there were some telephones that had higher added value and greater distinctiveness: unusual 'designer telephones', eg a telephone contained inside a cartoon character. These sold at higher prices, eg. US$85–200 (UK£50–120), and had higher profit margins. But distribution and sales depended on the whims of the major store buyers in large retail shop chains deciding to pick that product.

Office market

Another major source of sale for telephone handsets was through commercial and government contracts. As telephone office networks were modernised across the EC, new telephones were often installed, along with other telecommunications equipment such as telephone exchanges, private circuits and data networks. Telephone handset orders could be substantial for a small company, though they only formed a small part of the total investment in the new telecommunications network.

The primary contractor for most new telecommunications networks was often one of the large EC telecommunications equipment companies: Alcatel (France), Siemens (Germany) or Ericsson (Sweden) were the three largest in 1988.[2] Some of these companies subcontracted out such items as the telephone handsets because they were peripheral in sales and profits to their main activities. This presented opportunities for smaller telephone handset companies, but they needed to consider how they would market themselves to the large telecommunications equipment companies.

In addition, as Irish Telephones had discovered in the UK, there were other ways of marketing to the office market: office suppliers selling a range of equipment were willing to display telephone handsets as part of their comprehensive service to their customers.

CASE QUESTIONS

1. What strategy options would you advise the Irish company to pursue with regard to its current position and its European objectives?

2. What entry options would you wish to investigate for countries in the EC?

REFERENCES

1. European Commission *Panorama of EC Industry 1990*, OPOCE, Luxembourg, p 12–19 *et seq*.
2. European Commission *Panorama of EC Industry 1991/92*, OPOCE, Luxembourg, p 12–22.

8

The battle for the European breakfast cereal market*

In 1989, two of the world's largest food companies, Nestlé (Switzerland) and General Mills (US), decided to challenge the dominant European breakfast cereal manufacturer, Kelloggs (US). By 1992, the battle was fully joined. We look at the strategies employed and explore the issues raised.

MARKET BACKGROUND

The European breakfast cereals market was worth around US$3 billion in 1992. It grew around +10 per cent by value between 1991 and 1992. As Table 8.1 shows, the market has two distinct geographic areas: the UK breakfast cereal market, which accounted for almost half European consumption in 1992, and the rest of the European Community (EC). While the UK is much larger, it was the rest of the EC that was growing faster in 1991/2.

Table 8.1 European breakfast cereals market

	Market size 1992 By value (US$ billion)	Growth 1991/2
UK	1.4	+7%
Germany	0.35	+14%
France	0.25	+25%
Spain	0.1	+15%
Italy	0.05	+5%
Other	0.85	
Total	3.0	+10%

Source: Trade estimates and Aldersgate Consultancy

*This case was prepared from published data and private survey information. © Copyright Aldersgate Consultancy Limited 1993.

Most European breakfast cereals were eaten cold with milk, cornflakes and muesli being typical examples. Out of the total market in 1991 by value, it was estimated that under 5 per cent was eaten with hot milk: an example is hot porridge (a hot cooked oat cereal, served with sugar in England and salt in Scotland).

Although full global statistics on breakfast cereal consumption are not available, it is probable that the UK has the highest consumption per head in the world. The British eat even more per head at 13.3 lb per person per year than US citizens at 10.1 lb. Cereal consumption per head is much lower elsewhere in Europe: for example, in France it is just 1.8 lb per head.[1] For the future, it was not anticipated that general European consumption would reach UK levels. But substantial growth was likely, thus making the European market attractive to new entrants. One estimate was that the European would more than double by the year 2000 to a total size of US$6.5 billion at 1992 prices.[1]

EUROPEAN MARKET SEGMENTS

Because of the size and relative maturity of the UK breakfast cereals market, it is useful to examine this separately.

UK market segments

In the UK, growth over the years 1987 to 1992 has come primarily as customers have traded up from basic cereals like cornflakes to more healthy cereals such as muesli: the latter had higher prices and contained more expensive ingredients like nuts and dried fruit. Market research had shown that the basic market could be split into three main segments: staple products, healthy products and children's products. With increased consumer consciousness about health and appearance during the 1980s and 1990s, it was the health segment that had shown the most growth. The size of the main UK segments is shown in Table 8.2.

Table 8.2 UK breakfast cereals market: main segments

Segment	Typical products	1991 value By volume ('000 tonnes)
Staple products	Kelloggs Cornflakes, Weetabix, Shredded Wheat	160
Healthy products	Raisin Bran, All-Bran, Alpen Muesli	120
Children's products	Honey Nut Flakes, Coco Pops Rice Krispies	80
Other		50
Total		410

Source: Trade estimates and Aldersgate Consultancy

European market segmentation outside the UK

The extent to which UK segmentation might be repeated across Europe had not been resolved. However, there were a number of factors suggesting that other European markets might not be so different:

- the publicity for the single Europe;

- the willingness of young people across Europe to trial new and international products for themselves;

- the success of international branding;

- the general convenience of cold breakfast cereals;

- increasing numbers of working women across Europe;

- the trends towards healthy eating in the EC.

All the above factors indicated that European segmentation might be similar to the UK by the year 2000. However, there was no evidence that consumption per head would reach UK levels.

EUROPEAN MARKETING STRATEGY BASED ON MARKET SEGMENTATION

For new market entrants across Europe, one important strategy issue was to decide whether to attack each segment or concentrate on one only. Some specialist companies, such as the UK family-owned Jordans of Holme Mills, have concentrated on the healthy segment with organic quality ingredients at premium prices. The advantage of segmentation is that efforts can be concentrated to gain and sustain distribution in that part of the market. The disadvantage is that some parts of the market are thereby ignored.

In general terms, strategy also has to take into account the resources available to the company. When the two partners to the new joint venture, Nestlé and General Mills, were seeking new products in 1990, the market segment chosen was partly influenced by products already being made by the two companies elsewhere in the world. 'Cheerios' were already being made in the USA by General Mills and was one of their most successful products: it was taken virtually unchanged and launched into the European children's segment by the joint company in 1992 under the Nestlé brand name.

This process had the advantage of shorter development lead times and much lower capital commitment than would have been involved in developing a product from its inception. The disadvantage is that the product might not be suitable for national tastes outside America without a change in formulation which would defeat the objective of shortening the lead time.

PRODUCT PROFITABILITY IN BREAKFAST CEREALS

Although breakfast cereals use low added value raw materials such as wheat, oats and sugar, there are considerable costs involved in sophisticated packaging techology, product development, marketing and plant investment. Profits are therefore dependent on achieving and sustaining high volumes.

As a consequence, barriers to entry are also high. When putting together the joint venture in 1989, both Nestlé and General Mills contributed around US$80 million each to the deal.[1]

DISTRIBUTION AND PROMOTIONAL SUPPORT

European breakfast cereals are largely distributed through grocery outlets. Thus the large supermarket chains, such as Sainsbury (UK) and Carrefour (France), account for the bulk of sales. Marketing strategy has to address such important customers' needs if it is to gain distribution and be successful.

Grocery distribution is highly concentrated in many leading EC countries, as can be seen in Figure 8.1. This trade structure means that it is essential to persuade the leading grocery chains to stock and display the product.

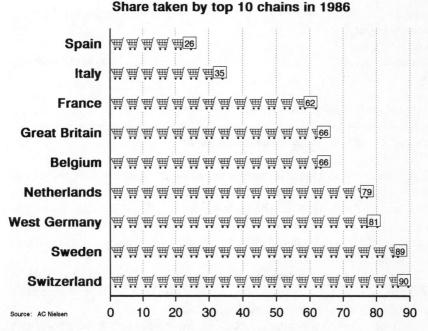

Figure 8.1 Concentrated European grocery buying

Nestlé is a European market leader in grocery products[2] with excellent distribution across Europe. Using Nestlé contacts and experience, the new joint venture partners were successful in gaining acceptance of their product range across the EC: by the end of 1992, grocery distribution of at least two products from the new range was over 80 per cent by value in the UK, France, Germany and the Benelux countries.

In accepting a product for listing, grocery supermarket chains find the projected level of advertising and promotional support persuasive. Typical levels of promotional support in European markets for major products would involve an advertising to sales ratio of 10 per cent during the introductory phase. In addition, there would be on-pack offers and price reductions. More details of actual activity are given below.

EUROPEAN COMPANY MARKET SHARES AND BRANDS

In 1992, Kelloggs dominated the European breakfast cereals market. It had a market share in excess of 50 per cent in all the main EC countries.[3] Overall brand share estimates for 1992 are shown in Table 8.3.

Table 8.3   European company market shares

	1992 market share (%) By value	
Kelloggs	60%	
Weetabix	6%	mainly in the UK
Cereal Partners*	8%	
Quaker Oats	4%	
Own Label	15%	mainly in the UK
Other	6%	

* The European company formed by Nestlé and General Mills

Source: Trade estimates and Aldersgate Consultancy

Kelloggs has over 30 brands in Europe: these range from Kelloggs Cornflakes, which alone has 15 per cent of the market, to Fruit'n'Fibre and Coco Pops. As new trends have emerged, it has launched new products. Kelloggs has made no concessions to European language in developing its main brand names: 'Fruit'n'Fibre' appears as the main pack name in the UK, Germany and Scandinavia, even though the wording is distinctly English.

All Kelloggs products are well supported by extensive TV advertising and by its strong franchise with European grocery outlets: no European supermarket chain could really afford to be without Kelloggs products.

In addition to growing the market, Kelloggs has steadily been gaining share over the years 1986–92. It took that share in particular from the second and third companies in the market place. Kelloggs is also market leader in the US with 38 per cent market share, General Mills being in second place with 25 per cent share.

Weetabix is a private company that has a business association with Whitworths, who sell dried fruit and cooking ingredients. Weetabix acquired Ready Brek from Allied Lyons plc in 1990 and has sales largely confined to the UK.

Cereal Partners is the 50/50 company formed by Nestlé (Switzerland) and General Mills (US) to attack the European breakfast cereal market. It bought the traditional UK product Shredded Wheat in 1990 from another company. Beyond this, it launched further products into Europe, but they were so recent that the brand shares shown in Table 8.3 would not reflect this activity.

Own label products are those made to the specification of major retailers under their own retail brand names. Cereal Parters and Weetabix are main manufacturers. Kelloggs does not undertake any own label work. The products tend to copy those of the market leaders.

THE JOINT VENTURE IN EUROPEAN BREAKFAST CEREALS

Clearly, with an entrenched competitor in Kelloggs, any company proposing to enter the market must be prepared for a long haul and substantial investment. Nestlé is one of the world's largest food companies with interests ranging from Nescafé instant coffee to frozen food under the Findus label. It has great marketing experience and resources. The company was reported to have been interested in the breakfast cereals market worldwide and to have investigated acquiring either Kelloggs or Quaker in the US as part of this ambition. But the price premium would have been high. Instead, Nestlé formed a global 'strategic alliance' in 1989[3] with the US company, General Mills (GM). The latter had the technology and spare production capacity for initial European production. It also had some major US brands such as Golden Grahams and Cheerios which it had been exporting to Europe on a limited scale for some years previously.

Given the complementary resources of the two partners, it is not surprising that they came together in 1989. The agreement operates in all markets except the US and Canada. The Nestlé manufacturer's name will appear on all products outside north America with either GM or Nestlé individual brand names as the lead for each product.

As far as Europe is concerned, the precise share ambitions of Cereal Partners are to obtain 20 per cent market share by year 2000.[1]

THE BATTLE FOR THE EUROPEAN MARKET

Cereal Partner's first task in 1990 was to establish a significant market presence in the UK. Thus the 'Shredded Wheat' name and production facilities were acquired from RHM Foods for around US$180 million in 1990. There was no change in the pack or product, except to introduce the brand name Nestlé as the manufacturer in the top left-hand corner. Kelloggs made no direct response to this move since it was already well positioned against this product in the UK. However, Cereal Partners then launched a series of new products and here the Kelloggs reaction was rather different.

In May 1991, Golden Grahams were launched by Cereal Partners (CP): it was a unique product, with heavy TV advertising support and a UK retail price of £1.39* for 375 g pack. Kelloggs immediately countered by relaunching its Golden Crackles product, similar but not the same as CP; it priced its product at £1.05* for 375 g pack including a '15 per cent extra free' offer. Kelloggs made sure its product was shelved in-store right alongside its rival.

In early 1992, CP launched its second product, this time aimed at the young children's market: Lucky Charms. The product was made from oat grain cereal and, new to Europe, crispy mallow pieces. However, it was entirely predictable to Kelloggs who had seen Lucky Charms launch in the US in 1965 and subsequently become the top children's cereal. Thus Kelloggs were able to respond by reformulating Ricicles to include similar mallow pieces. When CP launched their product with sample packs at 19p* Kelloggs responded by an introduction at 15p*. CP announced to the marketing press in January 1992 that they would be supporting Lucky Charms with £4.5 million (US$7.7 million) TV advertising in the UK alone.

In May/June 1992, CP then brought out Clusters: 'crisp wholewheat flakes with crunchy nuggets of almonds, pecans and walnuts' at a price of £1.59* for 375 g and further TV support. Kelloggs responded with a special offer on Golden Oatmeal Crisp 'slightly sweetened oat and rice flakes with raisins and almonds' consisting of 33 per cent extra free coupled with a price of £1.39* for what amounted to 500 g.

In addition, CP repackaged Cheerios under the Nestlé label and started introducing it into UK store distribution to replace the US General Mills product already available. In early 1993, CP changed the formulation of Cheerios to four different kinds of cereal rings: it must have been difficult to manufacture but would produce a real product edge against any counter-attack by Kelloggs.

The battle was well and truly joined!

---

* On-shelf prices are given for the UK launch in order to be specific about the activity at the time. Similar prices and deals were also being offered in other EC countries.

CASE QUESTIONS

1. What were the barriers to entry into the European cereal market in 1990?

2. How did Cereal Products overcome the barriers? What does the case suggest about the benefits of this move?

3. With each subsequent move by CP, why would Kelloggs respond immediately? Why not wait and see whether CP were simply wasting their resources against an entrenched competitor?

4. What significance do you place on CP launching innovative new products into the European market after their initial company purchase?

5. How important was the pricing activity and on-pack action of Kelloggs? Was it likely to prove effective against totally new products? And against heavy TV advertising to brand the new CP products?

6. Do you judge that CP will be successful in achieving their stated objective for the year 2000? Why?

REFERENCES

1. Knowlton, C (1991) 'Europe cooks up a cereal brawl' *Fortune*, 3 June, p 61.
2. Lynch, R (1990) *European Business Strategies*, p 66, Kogan Page, London.
3. Salier, J E (1991) *The General Mills Board and Strategic Planning*, Harvard Business School Case, p 12.

9

North American entry strategies for Eastern European markets*

Following the collapse of Communism and the command economies of Eastern Europe, many North American companies have identified this area as a major marketing and business opportunity for the 1990s. This case tracks market entry methods for some of these companies. It highlights some of the opportunities and problems encountered, including some that were rather unusual.

PROCTER & GAMBLE'S ENTRY TO THE CZECH AND SLOVAK DETERGENTS MARKET

With total sales of over US$24 billion, Procter & Gamble (P&G) is one of the world's largest consumer products companies. Brands include Ariel washing detergents, Pampers diapers (nappies) and Oil of Ulay skin moisturiser.

Although US sales still accounted for 62 per cent of its sales in 1990, P&G had been active in international development for many years. With total sales of over US$24 billion, it was already a major global company.

The company's international marketing strategy is based on:[1]

- heavy branding with truly international brand names, eg Ariel detergent powder and liquid, Crest toothpaste, Oil of Ulay skin moisturiser;

- policy of outspending the competition on major advertising media for its major brands;

- product performance that is demonstrably superior to competitors;

- highly motivated and professional sales team.

P&G's main global competitors in detergents are Unilever (UK and Netherlands), Colgate Palmolive (US) in some markets and Henkel (Germany) in some Euro-

---

pean markets. None of its competitors has pursued international branding with the single-mindedness of P&G.

In January 1991, P&G acquired the leading Czechoslovak detergent company, Rakona, for US$20 million.[2] Its new subsidiary held a virtual market monopoly in what has subsequently become the Czech Republic, as well as a major share in Slovakia. In addition to the purchase price, P&G also agreed to spend another US$24 million upgrading the Czech plant over the following four years. The concept of local monopoly brand share was perhaps misleading in the sense that it was agreed that P&G would also introduce new premium price Western brands over time: specifically Ariel, which was the largest selling washing product in Western Europe.

When compared to existing Rakona sales of only US$17.5 million, P&G's expenditure of US$20 million on existing plant and another US$24 million on new investment might appear extraordinarily generous. However, P&G intended the plant to serve as the main production source for Slovakia, Poland and Hungary, as well as the Czech Republic: Rakona is close to the Polish border but also has connections to the only Czech motorway, which leads down to Bratislava in Slovakia and on to Budapest in Hungary. P&G considered that cross-border trade with other Eastern European countries was essential to achieve the necessary economies of scale.

This judgement about the future of Eastern European trade was very different from that of P&G's rival, Unilever. The British and Dutch company took the view that exports from one Eastern European country to another would still be subject to significant tariffs for some years.[3] After studying Eastern Europe for two years, Unilever invested seperately in Poland, the Czech and Slovak Republics, and Hungary. It believed that national companies were required because:

1. this avoided import duties across Eastern European borders which could be as high as 40 per cent;

2. they allowed the acquisition of market share more quickly through the purchase of national companies rather than building share laboriously from a common base;

3. the economies of Eastern Europe could not sustain heavy imports and the countries would therefore discourage cross-border trade.

4. national company presence indicated national company commitment to each country in Eastern Europe.

Thus Unilever acquired companies in each country where it could across Eastern Europe. Its biggest purchases were in Poland and Hungary in 1991 with a Czech soap and detergents business being purchased in 1992.[4] In total, Unilever expected to invest over US$200 million to the end of 1992. Sales from companies acquired were estimated to be US$ 300 million at this time and would grow to to US$1 billion in 1997, if targets were achieved. Such rates of sales growth for consumer goods were quite exceptional by Western company standards.

Procter & Gamble was also investing heavily, especially in marketing funds to build brand franchise and brand share. While it remained to be seen which company strategy would be the most successful, P&G's strategy depended crucially on tariffs being lowered during the 1990s. The company must have therefore been encouraged in late 1992: Eastern European countries agreed to set up a regional trade zone designed to eliminate trade barriers gradually:[5]

- agriculture and industrial goods between 1995 and 1997;

- cars, textiles and steel by 2001.

In the intervening period up to 1995 at least, there would still be significant tariffs and national sensitivities about cross-border trade.

TAMPAX ENTRY INTO THE MARKETS OF THE FORMER USSR

Even after its new Ukranian plant came into operation, the major US company Tambrands estimated that it would still only supply 2 per cent of the potential market for tampon products: it owned the famous global brand Tampax.

In 1988, Tambrands invested US$10 million for a 49 per cent shareholding in a joint venture with the Soviet Pharmeceutical Ministry. The company was called Femtech and made tampons primarily for the former USSR market. As trade and investment liberalisation occurred, the US company subsequently acquired 100 per cent of the company.[6] At the same time, there were fundamental political changes taking place that severely affected the marketing environment.

- The Ukraine set up as a separate State with borders to the other former Soviet republics and a desire for its own currency.

- The Soviet Ministry ceased its functions: the product was no longer automatically distributed by a command economy to pharmacies all over the USSR. It needed to be marketed to the 15 independent states of the CIS.

- Inflation leapt from 2 per cent in 1989 to an estimated 2000 per cent in 1992 in the newly independent States, especially the Ukraine.[7]

Tambrands had to develop an entry strategy that coped with these changes. For technical reasons, it brought in production plant from the West: two lines were initially installed, with another added later and a fourth in 1992. The strategy was to fund these imports by hard currency exports of finished Tampax products into hard currency markets in the West. Beyond this, roubles earned from USSR sales were used to pay for all USSR raw materials and labour. Essentially, expansion was generated without recourse to international currency beyond that generated by the company itself. In 1992, the profits were used to purchase a factory site in St. Petersburg, Russia, and two more production lines. Key future managers were then sent to the UK for training.

Coping with hyperinflation was another major problem. Every month during 1992, the Ukranian chief accountant checked local supermarket prices and wage changes in the area. Factory wages of Tambrand employees were then raised accordingly. Equally, pricing and trading of tampons in the Ukranian market was also a major difficulty: recommended retail prices are meaningless when the average monthly price rise is over 50 per cent. There are no easy strategic solutions but hard currencies, such as the US dollar, and bartering arrangements were both used to overcome the problem.

In spite of the difficulties, the company was still profitable: by 1993, it was planning to use the profits to lease local Ukranian land around its factory in Kiev and build apartments for its workforce. In later years, Tambrands expected to be able to sell the flats, but this would depend on a clarification of the ownership law in the Ukraine.

THE LAUNCH OF PROCTER & GAMBLE'S 'WASH & GO' IN POLAND

In August 1991, Procter & Gamble (US) launched its market-leading shampoo Vidal Sassoon's 'Wash & Go' into Poland. At that time, the company was already the largest advertiser in the country. It was entirely consistent to arrange a major marketing campaign[8] for its new premium priced shampoo that included:

- mass-mailing free samples;

- a tour of Poland by Vidal Sassoon, the UK hairdresser;

- major distribution drive;

- heavyweight TV advertising, adapting the campaign that had already been used successfully in the West.

By the end of 1991, 'Wash & Go' had become the market leader in Poland with over one-third share of the shampoo market. Early in 1992, sales suddenly started falling: the reasons are still unclear, beyond the fact that there was absolutely nothing wrong with the product. Some possible explanations were as follows.

- Poland has had a reputation for being both enthusiastic for Western products but also deeply suspicious of commercial market forces.[8, 9, 10]

- A Polish research study found that three times more Poles disliked P&G's TV commercials than liked them. However, P&G's approach in the West has always been to design a campaign for sales effectiveness rather than entertainment value.

- The product itself was imported from the West rather than being manufactured in Poland.

- There was even a whispering campaign that the product caused dandruff and hair loss.[8]

- There was also some suggestion that the product, which was originally developed for the US practice of daily shampooing, may have been too sophisticated for Polish customers' cleaning needs.

Procter & Gamble countered quickly. It commissioned a public survey of Polish attitudes to its products early in 1992. The results were then sent to all wholesalers and retail stockists in May 1992. A covering letter pointed out that the product had undergone 150 000 hours of clinical tests and 250 million people around the world used the product.

The company also mounted a newspaper campaign presenting the product alongside its other well-known Polish brands, Ariel detergent and Pampers baby diapers (nappies). In addition, P&G's company president visited Poland to confer with Polish President Lech Walesa, about the possibility of local production. By 1993, share was beginning to build again.

US WEST TELEPHONE SERVICES TO CZECH AND HUNGARIAN MARKETS

US West is one of America's seven regional telephone companies. Like the other US telephone companies, anti-competitive laws in the US have encouraged it to seek growth outside America alongside its US ambitions. With annual capital expenditure totalling around US$2.5 billion, US West has substantial resources for overseas expansion.

The company has been seeking Eastern European expansion opportunities for several years. By 1993, it had landed two useful contracts in that area. They were quite small compared to its overall resources, but they could be seen as a method of gaining market entry and experience for larger deals later.

As background, Western help is needed to modernise Eastern European telephone systems: in 1993, waiting times for domestic telephones were 12 years in Hungary, 11 years in Poland and 10 years in the Ukraine.[11] The Organization for Economic Cooperation and Development (OECD) estimated that US$50 billion was needed to bring the service up to Western standards, excluding the former Soviet Union. The EC through its PHARE (Poland and Hungary Assistance Reconstruction Economic) programme, the European Bank for Reconstruction and Development and the World Bank have all made loans available, though to nothing like the OECD estimate above. Entry methods in this type of market therefore need to take into account government involvement, and also the availability of EC and international banking funds.

In Hungary, US West contracted in 1991 to build a mobile nationwide cellular telephone network in partnership with the government.[12] The capital cost was expected to be around US$50 million.

In the Czech Republic in 1992, the company was in the process of installing a major ground telephone network over a five-year period[11] at cost of US$80 million. This latter contract was obtained after a competitive bidding and assessment process by the former combined Czech and Slovak telephone authority. When the Czech and Slovak states went their separate ways in late 1992, Slovakia then decided to reconsider earlier network proposals that had been rejected in the bidding process from Germany's national telephone company, Deutsche Telekom. US

West would be the loser if these arrangements were adopted: political uncertainty would thus significantly affect US West's earnings from this venture.

US West was not the only American telephone company seeking Eastern European opportunities. The largest US telephone service provider, AT&T, has also had some success in developing Eastern European contracts: it provided US$58 million in 1991 to the Ukranian telephone company. In exchange in 1992, it took a 19.5 per cent share in the company.

But all the above deals are relatively small. Bigger contracts may well come if Eastern European governments privatise their networks. Those international companies already assisting in the countries involved might justifiably consider that they have a higher likelihood of success in the privatisation process. However, such considerations will at best be subject to detailed and lengthy negotiations with existing Eastern European managers. At worst, the exposure if the political regime changes might be significant, though perhaps not to a company with the size of AT&T, which had US$63 billion sales in 1991.

CHEVRON OIL IN KAZAKHSTAN

After some five years of intermittent negotiations, Chevron Oil (US) signed a deal in 1992 with President Nursultan Nazarbayev for rights to drill in the huge Tenghiz field in Kazakhstan: the field is conservatively the same size as the major field in Alaska's North Slope.[13, 14] One of the early problems was dealing with bureaucrats in Moscow who had made several attempts to destroy the deal because it would strengthen the national governments against the centre.

After the Russian coup in the summer of 1991, the Chevron senior managers firmly focused their discussion on Kazakhstan itself. This proved successful but there were still major difficulties. Because the government had never negotiated a large-scale contract of this kind before, there was little previous experience to draw on. The discussions were therefore longer and more painstaking than might have occurred elsewhere.

More generally, negotiation problems encountered by US and European companies in the former USSR have included the following.

- The need for a basic explanation of such basic Western concepts as profit and loss, risk and reward. Parts of the former USSR are still locked into Communist concepts from a previous era.[15]

- The need to undertake negotiations at several different levels simultaneously: local councils, regional government and at national level.

By negotiating directly with the Kazakhstan deputy prime minister, Chevron were able to avoid some of the problems outlined above. However, the subsequent coup attempt in that country in 1992 only underlined the real risk to the company from signing an agreement with a leader who was later under threat.

Once the deal has been signed, events can still be unpredictable. After BP Oil (UK) had negotiated a similar deal in Azerbaijan in 1992, the police turned up and locked the offices of the managers of the satellite communications system used to communicate back to BP headquarters in the UK. The company was told that the government had decided to regulate communications. BP merely commented that it had seen similar pressures when developing oil rights in South America. No doubt Chevron would make a similar mature response if faced with the same difficulty in Kazakhstan.

CASE QUESTIONS

1. What are the main difficulties encountered in entering Eastern European markets? For each area, what marketing and more general management solutions are available to overcome the problems identified?
2. What problems would you regard as the most difficult to resolve? And which would have the greatest profit exposure?
3. How would you approach the issue of placing a limit on a company's risk as it enters new markets, yet seeking the real rewards to be gained from successful new ventures?

REFERENCES

1. Mead, G (1992) 'Procter seeks to excel with a new formula', *Financial Times*, 21 August, p 6.
2. Grenillard, A (1991) 'Soft soap and hard sell', *Financial Times*, 25 July.
3. de Jonquieres, G (1992) 'Cleaning up after Communism', *Financial Times*, 3 July, p 12.
4. de Jonquieres, G (1992) 'Unilever steps up European expansion', *Financial Times*, 7 May, p 29.
5. Bobinski, C (1992) 'Eastern European countries set up a trading zone', *Financial Times*, 22 December, p 3.
6. Robinson, A (1992) 'Corporate citizenship seen rising from the ashes', *Financial Times*, 14 September, p 12.
7. OECD (1992) *Economic Outlook Number 52*, December, p 123.
8. de Jonquieres, G and Bobinski, C (1992) 'Wash and get into a lather in Poland', *Financial Times*, 28 June, p 18.
9. *The Economist* (1991) 'Survey of business in Eastern Europe', 21 September, p 14.
10. Bobinski C and Robinson, A (1991) 'Poland's hero strikers fall from grace', *Financial Times*, 22 September, p 7.
11. Shetty, V (1993) 'Priming the primary networks', *Communications International*, February, p 37.
12. *The Economist* (1992) 'Finding their voice', 8 February, p 90.
13. Hofheinz, P (1991) 'Let's do business', *Fortune*, 23 September, p 30.
14. Buckley, N (1992) 'Bringing oil to troubled waters', *Financial Times*, 14 September, p 12.
15. Holden, N J (1992) 'Exchange & Mart', *Marketing Business*, May, p 19.

10

Jacobs Suchard UK expansion

In early 1989, one of Europe's largest chocolate confectionery and coffee companies, Jacobs Suchard SA, had to decide about a possible launch of a range of confectionery products into the UK. The considerations were part of its global strategy to extend its brands worldwide and, more specifically, part of its single Europe expansion programme.[1] This case records the decision needed.

JACOBS SUCHARD SA

In 1982, the two Swiss companies Tobler Suchard, in chocolate confectionery, and Jacobs, in coffee, merged to combine their food efforts across Europe. By 1988, the combined company had sales of SFr6382 million (US$4.4 billion) and had become increasingly ambitious. It had made the following acquisitions.

1986: Van Houten, Holland – chocolate confectionery.

1987: E.J.Brach, US – sugar confectionery.

1987: Cote d'Or, Belgium – chocolate confectionery.

1987: Du Lac, Italy – chocolate confectionery.

In 1988, it also attempted to acquire the UK company Rowntree Mackintosh but was unsuccessful against Nestlé SA (see below). Immediately after these acquisitions, Jacobs Suchard remained profitable with 16.3 per cent return on capital before tax and interest. It had around 83 per cent of its sales in Europe and only 5 per cent in its home country.

Its profitability derived from its particularly strong chocolate confectionery and coffee brands in France and Germany. The company had both the investment and the skills to produce quality products, coupled with aggressive marketing that concentrated on a few leading products.

By 1988, it was able to comment in its Annual Company Report:

---

*This case was prepared from published data sources only. © Copyright Aldersgate Consultancy Limited 1993.

In view of the market globalisation and the development of global brands, we will give priority to 'Lila Pause' (an ingredient bar covered in chocolate), 'I Love Milka' (boxed nut chocolates) and 'Nussini' (chocolate biscuit) under the global brand name 'Milka' (its main milk chocolate). We shall focus on the UK, Italy and Asia using Milka.

JACOBS SUCHARD: EUROPEAN EXPANSION INTO THE UK

In addition to plans to reduce its production plants from 22 to 6 over several years, Jacobs Suchard decided to continue actively its policy of European expansion. The second largest country for confectionery consumption was the UK, as can be seen in Figure 10.1. Jacobs Suchard believed it was under-represented there. Its first move in 1988 had been to bid for the UK chocolate and sugar confectionery company, Rowntree Mackintosh. However, it was outbid by one of Europe's largest food companies: its fellow Swiss competitor, Nestlé SA, who paid US$4.25 billion (£2.5 billion).

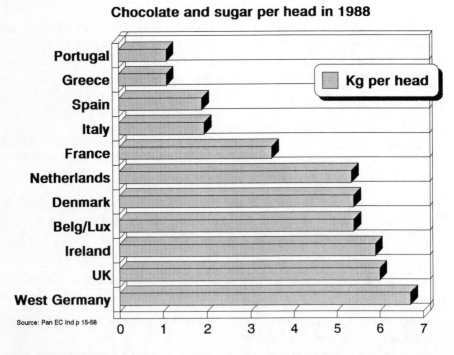

Chocolate and sugar per head in 1988

Kg per head

Portugal
Greece
Spain
Italy
France
Netherlands
Denmark
Belg/Lux
Ireland
UK
West Germany

Source: Pan EC Ind p 15-58

0 1 2 3 4 5 6 7

Figure 10.1 Confectionery consumption across the EC

Rowntree had a string of brands in the UK and also some brands that would be potential winners across Europe: 'Kit Kat' chocolate-coated bisuit, 'After Eight'

Table 10.1   1988 European confectionery market shares

	Jacobs Suchard	Rowntree Nestlé	Cadbury	Mars
UK	2%	29%	30%	24%
Germany	15%	11%	n/a*	22%
France	13%	27%	8%**	11%
Benelux	82%	2%	n/a	6%

*share not available but small
**share quoted before Cadbury's acquisition of Chocolat Poulenc later in 1988 – and you can see why

Source: *European Business Strategies*[2]

mint chocolates, 'Aero' aerated chocolate bars. For Jacobs Suchard, the particular attraction was that Rowntree was strong where Jacobs was weak: see Table 10.1. Having been unsuccessful with Rowntree, Jacobs Suchard now had to seek other ways to attack the UK chocolate market. To understand the options that were available, it is necessary to examine the UK chocolate market.

UK CHOCOLATE CONFECTIONERY MARKET

In 1988/9, the UK chocolate confectionery market was worth around £2.3 billion at retail selling prices. It was virtually static in terms of market growth.[3] Examining companies, there were three major competitors: Cadbury, Rowntree/Nestlé and Mars.

All three leaders had large chocolate manufacturing plant in the UK with extensive modern equipment. Equally, they had all been investing in their leading brands in the UK for many years and would typically spend £5–10 million per annum on advertising and promotional support for a leading brand. In addition, each of the three leaders had a large and highly professional salesforce. The three companies had strengths in different sectors of the massive chocolate market, as shown in Table 10.2.

JACOBS SUCHARD UK OPTIONS 1989

Jacobs Suchard already had a small presence in the UK through its well-known products Toblerone (a specialist chocolate and honey block) and Suchard boxed chocolates. However, both of these were relatively small. The company had been successful in a limited way with this policy. But, having been unable to take over Rowntree, it now needed to explore how it could extend its UK franchise. It has never publicly discussed its choices but, with such entrenched and formidable competitors, there were three main options.

Table 10.2 UK chocolate market: manufacturers' shares of segments 1988/9

	Countlines	Blocks
Rowntree	28%	28%
Cadbury	19%	51%
Mars	46%	8%
Total size (£m)	£1020 m	£310 m
Examples of brands:	Kit Kat	Cadbury's Dairy Milk
	Mars	
	Twix	Yorkie
	Marathon/Snickers	Galaxy
	Bounty	
	Milky Way	

Source: CTN News[3]
Note: A chocolate countline is a sweet bar made of items such as nuts, nougat, raisin or biscuit and coated in milk or plain chocolate. A chocolate block is a bar of solid milk or plain chocolate, sometimes with added pieces such as nuts and raisins.

1. To launch some specialist chocolate products that would not compete head-on with existing competition

Ferrero (Italy) had been highly successful in 1988 with the launch of its Ferrero 'Rocher' specialist boxed chocolates. Barker & Dobson (UK) had also been highly successful in 1984 with the launch of the 'Dime' chocolate countline from Marabou of Sweden. Both products were high quality, unique and well supported on TV media. In both cases, the companies had the great marketing strengths of being able to concentrate on one product launch. Not only did this mean well-targeted marketing and distribution effort, but the confectionery distributive trade was not asked to buy a whole range of products.

The top candidates in the Jacobs Suchard range were the 'Lila Pause' chocolate countlines: the differences from existing milk chocolate bars are described in the next section. Based on the launch of similar products, the best estimate of UK sales was £10–12 million pa for an advertising and promotion launch spend of £2–3 million.

2. To extend most of its European products directly into the UK

While this would build on its economies of scale and branding across Europe, there would be some duplication with what was already available in the UK from competitors. If it launched the whole range, its marketing effort would also be spread across a wide range of goods.

- Chocolate countlines under the 'Nussini' and 'Leo' labels: similar to others in the UK.

- Chocolate blocks under the 'Milka' label. These were of high quality but would directly compete against the UK market leaders Cadbury's 'Dairy Milk' and Rowntree's 'Yorkie'.

- Chocolate countlines under the 'Lila Pause' label. (A German name: it means 'Lilac Break' in English but it was not proposed to offer a translation.) The products were different in containing yogurt and muesli, along with high-quality chocolate and rice, but were not radically different from existing UK countlines.

Sales estimates were difficult for such a large range but one estimate was around £15–20 million at a launch cost of £5–8 million on advertising and promotions with a lower on-going level.

3. To acquire another UK chocolate or sugar confectionery company as a base for its UK expansion

Having been unsuccessful with Rowntree, Jacobs Suchard surveyed other potential UK candidates. The massive Mars company was too large and privately owned. The other major company was Cadbury–Schweppes which had well-known UK chocolate brands. It also had a well-developed international strong soft drinks franchise, but this would have been inconsistent with Jacobs Suchard desire to concentrate in its existing product areas. While this did not rule out Cadbury, the range of brands did suggest that the total cost of acquisition would be over £2 Billion.

There were three other candidates in the UK: the sugar confectionery companies, Trebor Sharp and Bassetts, and the Terry's Chocolate chocolate confectionery company. All three companies had well-developed marketing teams within the UK confectionery trade that would be able to drive distribution of Jacobs Suchard products.

However, Jacobs Suchard had some doubts about acquiring sugar confectionery companies, even when they were well entrenched in the UK market. These arose because it had been struggling since 1987 with its US sugar confectionery acquisition, E J Brach. It was in the process of cutting the number of product lines and reorganising this latter company.[1] Moreover, any sugar confectionery acquisition would not ostensibly fulfil its objective to develop global chocolate brands. Its problem with Terry's chocolate was that any acquisition would have bought market presence in the UK, but none of the economies of scale it was seeking.

Nevertheless, Jacobs Suchard would have examined the three possible acquisition candidates in depth.

1. Trebor Sharp claimed to be market leader in the UK sugar confectionery market with 13.5 per cent share and sales of £118 in 1988 including overseas activities. But, unlike chocolate, the UK sugar confectionery market was highly fragmented. Its products range from branded 'Extra Strong Mints' to semi-com-

modity sweets such as toffees. To acquire the company's assets and debts was likely to require over £100 million.

2. Bassetts had around 6 per cent of the UK confectionery market including its unique branded UK product: Liquorice Allsorts. The company also had a range of jelly sweets. Total sales were around £60 million including overseas activities. The cost of acquisition was reckoned to be in excess of £40 million.

3. Terry's chocolates had around 4 per cent of the UK chocolate confectionery market. It had some products that competed against the three market leaders, but its main products were in boxed chocolate selections, eg Terry's All Gold, where it had particular strengths. The company was a subsidiary of the UK company United Biscuits plc. The acquisition price was likely to be around £250 million to reflect its profits and strength in the UK market.

These were the main options open to Jacobs Suchard. The company had to decide which to pick.

CASE QUESTIONS

1. What are the advantages and disadvantages of each option? Which would you choose to attack the market? Why?
2. What would be your reaction to Jacobs Suchard's entry if you were one of the top three companies in the UK? What implications might this have for Jacobs Suchard in terms of its market entry strategy?

REFERENCES

1. Jacobs Suchard SA Annual Company Report, 1988.
2. Lynch, R (1990) *European Business Strategies*, p 47, Kogan Page, London.
3. CTN News, 9 February 1990, p 8.

11

Marketing the new European mobile cellular telephone network*

The new pan-European mobile cellular telephone network (called the GSM Network) was planned to start in 1992. For the first time, it would be possible for new mobile telephones to operate beyond their own national networks right across Europe.

But will the new system be a commercial success? Should it be marketed as one network across Europe or should each national European telephone network provider sell the new service as it chooses? And how should it be priced and promoted? This case sets out these issues as they stood at 1992. Whatever solution the telephone networks came up with, there could still be a better way of marketing the service. But what is that approach?

We will look at the evidence under five main headings and then draw some conclusions.

1. What is the pan-European mobile telephone cellular system?

2. European public service telephone total market.

3. Pan-European mobile cellular telephone market size and growth.

4. Pan-European mobile telephone market customers.

5. Pan-European mobile telephone marketing mix.

6. Conclusions.

WHAT IS THE PAN-EUROPEAN MOBILE TELEPHONE CELLULAR SYSTEM?

By the late 1980s, there were national mobile cellular telephone systems in a number of European countries, such as Britain, Germany, France and the Scandinavian countries. But, outside Scandinavia, the national systems for operating these net-

---

*This case was prepared from published data sources and private survey information.
© Copyright Aldersgate Consultancy Limited 1993.

works were incompatible. As a result of lengthy international technical discussions during the 1980s, a new pan-European system was agreed between the main network providers.[1] From 1992, new but not existing mobile telephones would be able to operate across many countries in Western Europe.

Mobile telephones allow the caller to use a mobile handset anywhere and not just from a fixed telephone point-and-socket to call other subscribers to the public service telephone network (PSTN). For example, the writer has used his handset 1000 m up a mountain in the northern English Lake District in a snow storm several kilometres from any normal telephone to make a call to a sunny English south coast.

The new network set up to achieve this is called 'cellular' because each mobile telephone broadcasts to a local transmitter/receiver. The national mobile network is made up of a number of transmitter/receiver cells, each of which is in turn linked to the fixed PSTN network. As the mobile telephone is used around the country, it moves automatically to a new receiver/transmitter and thus a new cell.

Cellular mobile telephones allow full voice communication while on the move. They are used typically by business and professional people who need ready access to a telephone, even when they are travelling. In general, the mobile service in each European country is provided by its main telephone service providers, such as France Telecom and Deutsche Bundespost Telekom, so we will look at these next. No organisation has been set up to provide a pan-European mobile service.

EUROPEAN PUBLIC SERVICE TELEPHONE TOTAL MARKET

The total market for all PSTN telephone services (including mobile services) was worth around 70 billion ECU in 1987. Turnover by country is shown in Figure 11.1. It was expected to grow to around 120 billion ECU in 1993:[2] the projected growth rate was around 9.5 per cent per annum, which was fast by any standards. By far the largest part of the market was accounted for by voice telephone traffic; mobile, data and fax activities were growing rapidly but would still only account for 4 per cent of the total telephone market in 1993.[2]

In over half the European Community (EC) countries, the main providers of telephone services were owned by their respective national governments.[3] More liberal market conditions operated in Germany, Finland and the UK. But even in this latter country, which had by far the most competitive market, there was a dominant supplier. The national companies had always found great difficulty agreeing common technical standards across Europe, let alone common services[4].

When it came to negotiating on the single Europe, some national companies fought hard to ensure that barriers to activity across Europe would only come down slowly after 1992. Ultimately, the main effect of the single Europe telephone service negotiations was to allow free competition in advanced telecommunications such as electronic mail and access to computer data bases from 1990. This would be followed in 1993 by competition in all basic data services. But voice telephone services would still be subject to national control.[4]

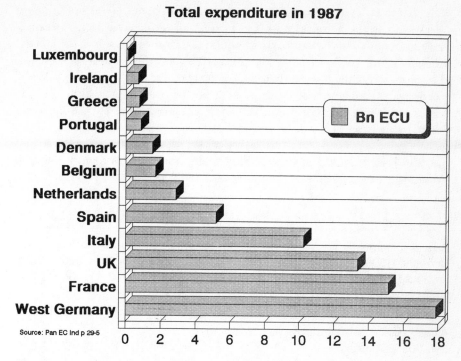

Total expenditure in 1987

Source: Pan EC Ind p 29-5

Figure 11.1 Public service telephone turnover

In terms of international activity in 1991/2, the main European PSTN companies were more concerned with setting up global telephone networks than promoting a pan-European mobile network.[5] This was because of the greatly increased global demand for telephone services, the very high profitability of international calls and the realisation that there was a unique strategic opportunity at that time to set up the first global telephone networks. Coupled with their experiences of negotiating any pan-European activity (see above), the opportunity for a mobile pan-European network did not appear to feature high in their priorities.

PAN-EUROPEAN MOBILE CELLULAR TELEPHONE MARKET SIZE AND GROWTH

The European mobile telephone service is part of the total European PSTN market described above. Mobile services were worth 2.4 billion ECU in 1989. They were expected to grow to 5.8 billion ECU by 1993 and then nearly double by 1999: a rate of growth of around 14 per cent per annum. While it would only represent a small part of the total telephone service market above, it would still be a substantial market in its own right.

Total market revenue was expected to come from two sources: sales of *equipment* to take part in the network and sales of *services* once connected to the network. Table 11.1 shows actual and projected figures for these two areas. It also shows the *total* number of mobile telephones installed up to 2000, though many of these will not be able to use the new pan-European system because they were made before it was designed. While precise estimates have not been given, it is likely that the number of mobile telephones capable of participating in the new pan-European system by the year 1999 will be around 5 000 000 *telephones*.

Table 11.1 Projected sales of cellular telephones and network sales in Western Europe 1990–2000 at constant 1990 prices

	1990	1992	1994	1996	1998	2000
Annual equipment sales						
By volume (000s)	850	1 050	800	880	1 220	1 560
By value (ECU million)	1 700	1 890	1 280	1 232	1 464	1 794
Total installed base of mobile telephones (year end)						
By volume (000s)	2 300	4 270	6 020	7 600	8 880	11 890
Annual service revenue across Western Europe						
By value (ECU million)	1 932	3 715	5 298	6 840	8 347	11 890

Source: Aldersgate Consultancy Limited

PAN-EUROPEAN MOBILE TELEPHONE MARKET CUSTOMERS

With the arrival of the single European market from 1 January 1993, it was anticipated that this would lead to significant demand for new pan-European mobile telephone services.[2] They would be particularly valuable for businesspeople operating across Europe. They might also appeal to others such as transport delivery drivers and sales personnel operating across several European countries: such people currently rely on a fixed telephone in an office, hotel or public call box which is not convenient for some types of call.

Inevitably, there is an element of speculation in the demand estimate above. While the technologists were devising the new European-compatible system, little market evidence was gathered on the level of demand for the new service. Indeed, the evidence that was available did not suggest a high level of cross-country activity. In early 1990, it was reported[6] that the Scandinavians (Norway, Sweden, Finland, Denmark) had offered mobile telephone compatibility for several years, not only between their own countries but also with Switzerland. But, in practice, they found that cross-country activity accounted for a small proportion of total activity: under 5 per cent in this period. However, this evidence referred to a period before the single Europe was a reality, so it was hardly conclusive.

Moreover, pan-European demand was expected to be much higher where mobile telephones were used close to several networks. For example, a mobile telephone in Ireland might have little cross-border activity because it is geographically remote, but a telephone in Belgium might have rather more being close to French, Dutch and German borders.

Demand would also depend on the extent to which the new service providers were willing to promote a pan-European network. Apart from the UK and Germany, Europe's mobile cellular telephone networks are operated solely by the national monopoly PSTNs in each country as part of their total telephone service. With their large existing investments to protect and in the absence of market competition, it would be understandable if these organisations wished to ensure that any mobile developments did not undermine their existing telephone business.

In the UK, Finland and Germany, the market situation was somewhat different for mobile telephones. Specifically, these had appointed a second mobile network operator beyond the dominant service provider: British Telecom's rival to its 'Cellnet' mobile operation (of which it owned 60 per cent) was 'Vodaphone' from Racal Telecommunications. After operating for some five years, Vodaphone had taken market leadership in the UK in terms of the number of subscribers.

In Germany, Mannesmann Mobilfunk was given approval in December 1989 to set up a rival to compete with the State-run Deutsche Bundespost Telekom.[7] Given the buoyancy of the German economy and wealth of the nation, it was expected that mobile telephones in Germany would make fast progress. However, as Table 11.2 indicates, the country had a long way to go to catch up with the European leaders in mobile telephones. The reason may well have been that the purchase of a mobile telephone in Germany in 1992 cost around US$3400, compared to the equivalent cost in the UK of around US$340 to 850 and in Italy around US$1050.

Table 11.2 Cellular telephone subscribers in Europe in 1990

	Subscribers	Population millions	Penetration as percentage population
UK	660 000	57.5	1.1%
Sweden	300 500	8.5	3.5%
Italy	266 000	57.6	0.5%
Norway	165 000	4.2	3.9%
France	140 000	56.5	0.2%
Finland	135 000	5	2.7%
West Germany	128 000	62	0.2%
Denmark	118 000	5.5	2.1%
No other European country had more than 50 000 subscribers			

Source: Trade estimates

PAN-EUROPEAN MOBILE TELEPHONE MARKETING MIX

All marketing promotion of the new pan-European mobile network would need to look hard at customer demand evidence. In some ways, the difficulty is that the

data are limited because the service is so new. In addition, the public service telephone network providers outside Germany and the UK did not inspire confidence
that they would enthusiastically support cross-European promotion. But there
were some hopeful signs.

Product

Some of the largest mobile telephone manufacturers in the world were now well
down the road of manufacturing the *equipment*.[8] NEC from Japan, Motorola from
the USA and Ericsson from Sweden were among those keen to supply and promote equipment for the new service. The Japanese had been unable to gain any
contracts for the telephone networks that would be needed. But it was anticipated
that they might repeat across Europe their UK success when it came to selling the
phones themselves: essentially, the Japanese manufacturers were low-cost producers
of telephones. They would produce cheap and reliable mobile telephones. The
strategy of some European competitors was to make product differentiated telephones that were lighter, had more facilities and used longer lasting batteries.

At least the product *equipment* issue was largely resolved. But what was not clear
at all in product marketing terms was the scope for a pan-European mobile *service*.
From 1992, there would be a series of new national mobile telephone services with
transmitters that would link with others when travellers crossed European borders.
The issue that was still open was whether market demand would be stimulated
more rapidly by continuing with these current national PSTN arrangements or
developing a service with its own brand that operated truly across Europe. Could
there be a new 'mobile Euronet' with all the branding and imagery that this might
provide?

Pricing

In order to operate *any* form of cross-European service, some cooperation between
national PSTNs had already been agreed, otherwise it would not have been possible
to charge customers for the service used once they had crossed a national border.
Essentially the agreement was that each mobile telephone would be registered in a
home country. When it was used outside that country, the new network would
charge the home country PSTN with the costs and these would then be passed
back to the subscriber.

Several additional pricing issues had also been resolved between the national
PSTNs.

1. There would be no common tariffs between PSTNs. This meant that price
    competition would be possible between networks covering the same area: this
    particularly applied to the UK and Germany. It also meant that there could be
    no common European network price at this stage.

2. The collection risk of obtaining the subscriber's money would be taken by the
    home service provider, who would add a handling charge of around 25 per

cent to the original call charge to cover this and other costs. Thus, a German network operator would bill its counterpart in the UK, who would then bill a UK telephone used in Germany adding a UK service fee.

3.   Although there will be price competition between national networks inside a country and no fixed pan-European price, cross-country handling charges were fixed to stop an individual registering a mobile telephone in the cheapest country in order to avoid paying higher prices elsewhere in Europe.

While the lack of a common price agreement might make a truly pan-European service more difficult to achieve, it does not necessarily rule out the service: many products across Europe charge different prices in different countries. What is important about the above agreement on tariffs is that the PSTNs have been able to agree clear pricing arrangements to charge customers anywhere in Europe.

Actual prices in 1992 for a national mobile service worked out about the same as international European calls. Table 11.3 gives an example from the UK.

Table 11.3 Telephone prices in UK

Prices for 1 minute of peak time: UK£ spring 1992			
Local	National UK	Mobile UK	International in EC
0.1	0.2	0.4	0.4

With the added 25 per cent for handling, a mobile call inside another European country is likely to work out more expensive than an international call from a fixed telephone to that country. But this was never a real issue for mobile telephone users: the *basic convenience* of using a mobile telephone has more than made up for the extra call costs.

Promotion

Because no truly pan-European service has been envisaged, no start-up promotional plans and costs have ever been devised. Undoubtedly, they would be significant across the whole of Europe, possibly rivalling the reputed £200 million spent on the pan-European launch of a grocery brand in 1991. A rolling European launch taking advantage of the European product life cycle might be one way of concentrating on the most productive markets and providing better control of the launch in the early years.

Place

As discussed above, this would depend on the home country of the mobile telephone. Beyond this, the issue of pan-European mobile telephone coverage remained to be resolved.

CONCLUSIONS

The basic agreements between the PSTNs to run a pan-European cellular mobile telephone network had been resolved. The telephone equipment to operate the network was expected to be in place from around 1992. National network service providers would be selling the pan-European advantages of their telephones as part of their planned development of their mobile telephone network.

But the possible demand for a truly pan-European network had not been tested. The marketing challenge of setting this up had never been truly investigated and resolved. There would be formidable difficulties in the face of the national telephone company interests. But the reward would potentially be the largest mobile telephone network in the world.

CASE QUESTIONS

1. What were the reasons for the slower growth of mobile telephones in some European countries?

2. Why might the national telephone networks be reluctant to implement the new pan-European mobile network?

3. In spite of the difficulties, what marketing mix would you recommend for the development of a pan-European mobile system? Would there be any benefit in gaining the support of the European Commission for such a package?

REFERENCES

1. *Communications International* (1989) 'Test solutions for the GSM', December p 43.
2. European Commission, *Panorama of EC Industry 1990,* OPOCE, Luxembourg, p 30–8.
3. Lynch, R (1990) *European Business Srategies*, pp 238–9, Kogan Page, London.
4. *Financial Times* (1989) 'Untangling Europe's telecommunications networks', 11 December, p 5.
5. *Financial Times* (1991) 'Top telecommunications companies consider global deal for business', 5 April, p 1.
6. Zehle, S (1990) 'The key to EC Cellular', *Communications International*, January, p 41.
7. *Financial Times* (1989) 'West Germany's telephone network poised for big expansion', 8 December.
8. *Financial Times* (1989) 'Wrangles hit flagship project', 19 September.

12

European car pricing*

According to the UK Monopolies and Mergers Commission's 1992 study of small cars in Europe, there are considerable variations in price between European Community (EC) countries.[1] These cannot be explained by currency differences, tax variations or extra equipment supplied on some models. They originate with the manufacturers themselves and their ability to maintain higher prices in some EC countries, principally the UK.

On medium and larger cars in Europe and taking into account the same factors, the study found that there was no significant difference in price levels between the same countries.

With the coming of the single Europe, should the car manufacturers expect to set the same prices across the EC? Should there be a pan-European pricing policy?

BACKGROUND

In both 1989 and 1990, the EC passenger market was larger than the USA. Sales in the EC amounted to around 12.4 million cars in 1990 with the UK entering a period of decline, but Germany, and to a lesser degree other EC countries, still showing significant growth. Figure 12.1 shows the sales per country. It was not until late 1992 that the EC market produced its first real drop in volume.

For many years, some European car companies such as Ford (US) have manufactured cars on a pan-European basis, eg its small car, named the 'Fiesta', combined parts produced in the UK, Germany and Spain in the finished model.[2] Other companies have essentially produced one model in one location, eg Volkswagen (Germany) has always produced its medium-sized Polo range only at its factory in Wolfsburg, West Germany. The cars were then shipped across the EC.

The EC car market is not truly pan-European in the sense that any model can be readily sold in any other country. There are detailed car and legal regulations in each EC country, eg yellow headlights in France and car emission standards in Germany, that effectively prohibited this happening. However, it was for precisely this reason that the Single Market Act 1986 was enacted: over time, it was envisaged that, apart from some obvious differences such as the British and Irish desire to drive on the left, car market standards would become the same. At this time, if not before, prices could surely become the same across Europe.

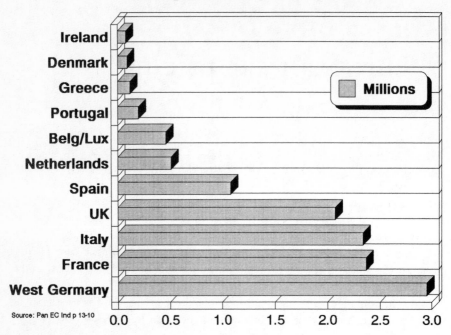

Car registrations by country 1990

Source: Pan EC Ind p 13-10

Figure 12.1 Motor vehicle sales in the EC

CAR PRICES ACROSS EUROPE

As champions of the European car customer, the Bureau Européene des Unions de Consommateurs (BEUC) has been campaigning for many years to bring down car prices in what is regarded as the expensive countries in Europe. BEUC is made up of the national consumer associations of most EC member countries. It produces surveys of car prices such as that shown in Table 12.1.

Table 12.1 New car prices across Europe

		Prices in ECU		
Car	*Denmark*	*Germany*	*France*	*UK*
BMW 316i	8 926	10 919	11 071	13 218
Citroen CX 22TRS	8 982	13 012	12 361	14 282
Fiat Tipo 1400	5 416	7 359	7 081	9 143
Ford Orion 1400	–	8 197	7 837	10 799
Renault 19	6 390	9 543*	9 493	11 310

* with catalytic converter

All prices per model, per country, net of taxes at June 1989

Source: BEUC

From the data in Table 12.1, there would appear to be large differences between prices in different countries. BEUC reported that average new car prices varied by 70 per cent between the lowest and highest countries net of tax. The difference including taxes was as much as 128 per cent. Since EC rules lay down that the maximum difference should only be 18 per cent, there was some concern expressed. It should be noted that the EC rules specifically exclude those countries with exceptionally high national taxes such as Denmark and Greece.

Perhaps not surprisingly, some 200 000 cars had been brought into the UK by individual buyers between 1980 and 1985, mainly from Belgium. The car manufacturers were reported to be concerned that this undermined their profitability.[3]

According to BEUC, the basic reason for these price differences was that the manufacturers were taking advantage of a system of exclusive dealerships in EC countries. These effectively meant that manufacturers could stop shipping cars to any dealer if they were then sold to nationals of another country.

The manufacturers argued that there were a number of other major reasons for the differences in price between EC countries: different tax systems, exchange rate variations, different car specifications, different dealer discounts. It was not a question of 'what the market would bear'.

In 1984, the European Commission agreed a Block Exemption Regulation to exempt the passenger car industry from the Treaty of Rome rules on competition. Specifically, it allowed the motor trade to operate the system of exclusive distributor franchises so that they market supply in an area was controlled by the manufacturer. The reason given by the Commission for allowing this exemption was that motor vehicles are complex products and require a high level of after-sales service; this would be best served by allowing dealers to have exclusive rights in a geographical area.

With the exemption coming up for review in 1994 and the single European market becoming more established, the manufacturers will have to decide whether to seek a continuation of this policy. Perhaps they would be better to consider a pan-European pricing policy. But there were still real variations in other aspects of car marketing across Europe that could be reflected in prices.

REASONS FOR DIFFERING CAR PRICES ACROSS EUROPE

The real question is whether the reasons for the differences across Europe were sufficient to justify the absence of a pan-European pricing policy. We will examine the evidence under four headings:

- customers;

- tax variations;

- dealer arrangements;

- other areas.

Customers

As Table 12.2 shows, car ownership across the EC follows wealth only to a limited extent. It is distorted by such other factors as the availability of public service transport, the level of car sales taxes levied by the national government, and the likelihood of obtaining a car as part of a work pay and remuneration package. Table 12.2 also shows this latter area for selected countries.

Table 12.2 Car ownership across the EC

	GDP per head in 1989	Cars per 1 000 of population in 1989	% of senior managers with company cars 1991
West Germany	20 440	490	80%
Italy	15 120	426	75%
France	17 820	410	53%
UK	14 610	372	95%
Belgium	16 220	366	n/a
Netherlands	15 920	341	85%
Denmark	20 450	314	n/a
Spain	9 330	290	50%
Ireland	8 710	197	n/a
Portugal	4 250	193	n/a
Greece	5 350	128	n/a

Source: Panorama of EC Industry 1991/2, p 13–11, World Bank and Aldersgate Consultancy estimates

The claimed effect of variation across Europe in the provision of company cars has been to distort car prices: company fleet buyers purchase in large quantities; they are therefore able to obtain sizeable price discounts that are not available to the private buyer. In order to maintain their profits, car companies have to charge private buyers higher prices to keep their operations profitable. Higher prices for private buyers result.4

Tax variations

Table 12.3 shows that there are very substantial variations across the EC in taxes levied on cars. When making price comparisons across Europe, it is therefore essential to take into account the effective prices that are charged gross of tax.

When car manufacturers complained about price comparisons made by the consumer groups, one of their comments concerned this area.

Table 12.3 VAT and additional sales taxes on new cars

	VAT	Extra taxes in 1992
Belgium	25% up to 3000 cc 33% above	none
Denmark	22%	105% up to DK19 750 180% on rest
France	22%	none
Germany	14%	none
Greece	6%	45–400% depending on engine size
Italy	19% up to 2000 cc 38% above	
Luxembourg	12%	none
Portugal	17%	Esc 95–1700 per cc on increasing scale
Ireland	21%	21.7% up to 2016 cc 24.7% above
Spain	33%	none
UK	17.5%	10%

Source: Monopolies and Mergers Study UK, 1992

Dealer arrangements

Across Europe, car manufacturers have agreements with dealers in a geographical area for the sale of their product ranges. There are a number of restrictions placed on the dealers:

- limitations on the dealer's ability to advertise outside its franchise area;

- stop a dealer acquiring or holding dealerships outside the existing area from other suppliers;

- prevent the dealer acquiring or holding other dealerships except on a distinct and separate site;

- restrict the ability of the dealer to sell other products, such as second-hand cars or car parts from other manufacturers;

- limit the dealer to selling a maximum quantity of cars in a given period and to a maximum percentage of the total cars from the manufacturer in one year.

While all these restrictions limit dealer freedom, the car manufacturers have said that they do make it more likely that car service levels are of the highest quality. Moreover, European car companies are engaged in a fiercely competitive battle in any one EC country, so that the EC has accepted that these dealer restrictions are acceptable in terms of the EC Block Exemption Regulation.

Data have been published on the number of dealers that each of the main EC car manufacturers has in each country.[5] In general terms in 1991, manufacturers tended to have rather more dealers in the main country of manufacture, eg Renault in France, Rover in the UK. The Japanese car companies had rather fewer dealers, but this would be consistent with their overall share of the European car market at around 9 per cent in 1989.[6] The US multinationals, Ford and General Motors (trading as Opel in Germany and Vauxhall in the UK), were well represented in numbers of dealerships across Europe, reflecting their market share of 21 per cent.[6]

It should be noted that the *number* of dealers provides no indication of their *quality* in terms of location, size, trained staff, workshop facilities etc.

Other areas

As will be generally true in all pricing decisions, the costs of car production need to be reflected in the prices: there would be no point in pricing below marginal costs. In fact, such a pricing policy is illegal in some EC countries.

While European car manufacturers do not publish detailed comparative cost data for competitive reasons, outline data on wage costs by country are summarised in Table 12.4.[7]

Table 12.4 Wage costs in selected countries

1991 in Deutschmarks per hour

		Typical car companies
Germany	45	Volkswagen, BMW
Italy	32	Fiat
Spain	29	SEAT (Volkswagen/Audi group)
France	29	Renault
UK	29	Rover
And for comparison		
US	35	
Japan	34	

Source: German Auto Industry Association

Other areas that would need to be considered include the extra items added to some cars as standard, eg electric windows, in-car stereo systems, fuel injection. European car manufacturers have commented that this is the area that has made UK cars more expensive.

REASONS FOR NATIONAL PRICE DIFFERENCES IN 1991

To assist understanding of how prices are constructed and explain why some national prices are higher than others, the European car manufacturer General Motors commissioned a study of comparative prices in 1991. This is shown in Table 12.5. It demonstrates that significant differences can emerge from what is basically the same car.

Table 12.5 Comparative prices (1991 £s)

	UK Astra L1.4 5-door non-cat	German Kadett GL 1.4 5-door catalytic	France Kadett GL1.4 5-door non-cat
List price inc tax	8 749	7 407	7 764
List excluding tax	7 023	6 497	7 764
Equipment adjustments (EA)	–	482	257
EA list price excluding tax	7 023	6 979	6 468
Discounts from dealer	13.7%	7.1%	2.8%
On-road costs	350	152	314
On-road price ex tax	6 411	6 636	6 601
Financing support	672	160	–
On-the-road with finance	5 739	6 578	6 601

Source: GM Vauxhall 1991 Survey

Table 12.5 was constructed from what was claimed to be a detailed survey of the way customers actually make car purchases, ie by trading in an old model and taking out finance to purchase a new car.

CASE QUESTIONS

1. How should car prices be set in each EC country?
2. Should the car industry press the EC Commission to continue with Block Exemption after 1994?
3. Clearly there is currently no pan-European pricing policy, but should there *ever* be one across the EC? Or should the car companies continue with what are essentially national policies?

REFERENCES

1. Monopolies and Mergers Commission (1992) 'New motor cars', HMSO February.
2. Doz, Y. (1986) 'Strategic management in multinational companies', p 14, Pergamon, Oxford.
3. Griffith, J. (1991) 'Bad dreams return to the motor trade', *Financial Times*, 10 May, p 11.
4. *Financial Times* (1992) 'Market distorted by use of company cars as perks', 6 February, p 6.
5. Ibid.
6. European Commission (1991) *Panorama of EC Industry 1991/92* OPOCE, Luxembourg, p 13–10.
7. Fisher, D. (1992) 'Time to become lean and mean', *Financial Times*, 23 June, p 18.

13

Marketing mix for AlpenFerien*

In November 1992, Dieter Schmidt and his fellow director, Paul Hausmann, were reviewing their company, AlpenFerien GmbH, which operated walking and mountaineering holidays in the Bavarian Alps. The firm was their joint creation and had been successful for a number of years. But in 1992 there had been a struggle for survival. The two partners were the main employees of the company, which was based in the tourist centre of Garmisch–Partenkirchen, Bavaria.

COMPANY CUSTOMERS AND COMPETITORS

In past years, Germans had formed almost all the customers of the company. In the last two years, the proportion had declined to about 60 per cent with Italians, French and other Europeans replacing them. Fortunately, this new business had almost compensated for the loss of German customers with the total company turnover down only slightly over the previous year. But German inflation had moved ahead and it had therefore been difficult to make a small profit and, more importantly, take out an adequate salary.

Part of the problem was undoubtedly competition from other walking and climbing areas, particularly as Eastern Europe opened up. There was anecdotal evidence that Germans wanted to go further afield, for example to the Tatra Mountains on the Czech/Polish border. However, based on their own observation and data from the local tourist board, this was compensated by other Europeans coming in increasing numbers to the Bavarian Alps. Perhaps this is what was meant by the 'single Europe'.

AlpenFerien also faced direct competition from three other similar businesses in the immediate area and others just over the border in Austria.

COMPANY PRODUCT AND PRICING

Dieter and Paul's small business was based on mountain trips into the local mountains.

* This case was based on a real company whose identity has been disguised. © Copyright Aldersgate Consultancy Limited 1993.

They both had international mountaineering leadership certificates and had been operating the company for about five years. Dieter had in fact started it and brought in his friend Paul after a couple of years: they had been climbing partners since their student days. The company's season ran from May to September: before and after that, few tourists went up into the Bavarian Alps on walking tours.

Mountaineering trips on offer in southern Germany varied from simple one-day affairs in the lower valleys to major six-day trips staying overnight in mountain huts in the area. Some would involve walking using public footpaths but others would entail leaving public trails in order to climb easy peaks: equipment such as ropes, slings and climbing harnesses would be provided by the company in these circumstances.

After covering the area for some years, the two knew the most interesting routes well. They also knew that they had the facility to call on climbing and walking friends if demand was particularly high. But their experience was that this had not really happened and, in any event, they liked to keep the company small and friendly. Their expertise and knowledge was well known, and they had the support of the local and regional government travel agencies.

Dieter felt that the company had worked out the best range of trips or excursions over their five years of operation. There was little to be added without moving to a new base away from Garmisch–Partenkirchen. Not only would this have proved costly, but it would have moved the company beyond its present small and easily-controlled market. Examples of the price ranges for trips were as follows:

One-day valley walk: DM150* per person

Minimum of 8 people

Three-day mountain walk: DM500 per person plus overnight and meal costs of approximately DM100 per person for the three days

Minimum of 6 people

Six-day mountaineering peaks with overnights, meals, equipment and minibus back to base included: DM1250 per person

Maximum of 6 people

These prices were in line with those charged by other walking companies in the area.

COMPANY PROMOTION

Company promotion was kept very simple. Dieter and Paul knew that brochures were important for advertising the business. As far as German customers were concerned, a new leaflet was produced during the off-season and mailed out to previous customers, along with a personal letter signed by either Dieter or Paul. They also sent the same brochure to mountain and walking clubs that had visited

*DM2.45 = £1

the area, and put small advertisements in the columns of German walking magazines.

For other Europeans, the company relied on the local tourist office and hotels to make the initial contact. It appeared that people outside Germany were less familiar with the mountains and lakes of southern Bavaria than with other, more popular walking areas. Most of their customers outside Germany came as a result of seeing leaflets and brochures in the Bavarian Tourist Board offices or from hotels, camp sites and youth hostel accommodation. Because most of these people were touring the area, they tended to buy the one or three-day trips.

THE FUTURE

As their meeting continued, Dieter and Paul were speculating as to how they could obtain more customers from outside Germany. Specifically, they were wondering how they could attract customers from the rest of the European Community (EC). They knew that their service product was fine in itself and would be interesting to Europeans. They were also aware that there were plenty coming to the Alps, though relatively few came to Germany: rather more went to Switzerland, France and Austria.

Perhaps they should start talking with specialist walking tour operators in other EC countries that would bring interested groups to the Bavarian Alps. They had made some enquiries and discovered that European travel agents sought a commission of at least 6 per cent for all orders booked, which they felt the company could afford. Where tour operators provided a group of tourists, Dieter and Paul were willing to discuss a larger commission, possibly as much as 15 per cent. These larger discounts might be given if, for example, they formed a link with one of the specialist adventure travel operators, such as Exodus or Waymark in the UK.

CASE PROJECT

You have been approached by Dieter and Paul to develop a marketing plan for AlpenFerien to attract customers from elsewhere in the EC. The two partners had already collected some data relevant to such a plan: this is shown below. Specifically, the minimum objective would be to sell 200 trips in year one with an average length of three days at a target customer price of DM600.

The marketing plan needs to cover all aspects of the marketing mix and produce specific recommendations.

Alpen Ferien: Selected tours operating in the area

In the valley (from Garmisch): Grainauer Fussweg, Hammersbacher Fussweg, Sudl, Talweg, Schwaigwanger Fussweg, Loisach–Partnach Uferweg.

Up to 300m above the valley: Zugzpitz area, Geschwandtnerbauer, Pfeiffer–Alm.

Up to 1000m above the valley: Hohenweg from Bergstation, Hausberg Cable Car to Kreuzwankl.

Over 1000m above the valley: Kramerspitze, Krottenkopf, Meilerhutte, Schachenschloss, Osterfelderkopf, Alpspitze, Zugspitze.

Walking with the Tourist Office

From mid-June to mid-September, the Tourist Office arranges one-day guided hiking tours on Tuesdays and Thursdays. Specialist one-day walks with a botanical interest are operated every Wednesday during the same period. The destination for all tours depends on the weather and is announced one day in advance in the local Bavarian newspapers.

Data on holidays in Europe is shown in Figures 13.1, 13.2 and 13.3.

Holiday data for 1985

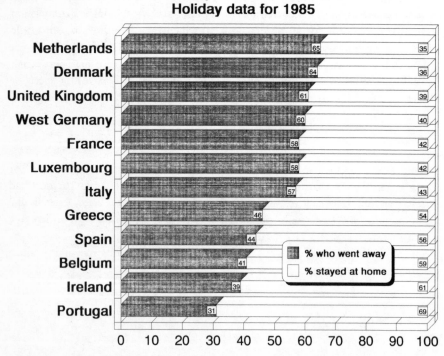

Figure 13.1 Europeans who went away on holiday

Source for Figures 13.1, 13.2 and 13.3: EUROSTAT (1991), 'A Social Portrait of Europe', Office for official publications of the EC, Luxembourg, pp 126–7.

Holiday data for 1985

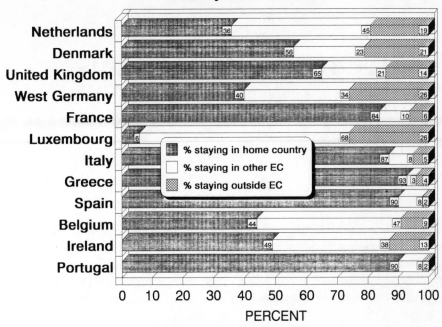

Figure 13.2 Countries visited during main holidays

Holiday data for 1985

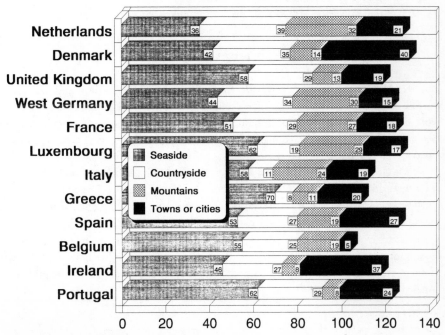

Note: Total over 100 due to multiple replies

Figure 13.3 Main holiday destinations

14

McDonalds Restaurants marketing mix across Europe*

One of the major marketing successes of the last few years has been the spread throughout Europe of McDonalds Restaurants (US). The company pioneered a totally new approach in Europe to high quality, standardised menu items, with fast and friendly service and strong branding. Restaurant openings in virtually every capital city across Europe confirm that the company has tapped into a true pan-European customer segment.

This case explores the reasons for this success. In particular, it examines:

- the nature of the pan-European customer;

- the extent to which McDonalds marketing mix is standardised across Europe.

COMPANY BACKGROUND

In 1992, McDonalds had a worldwide turnover of US$7133 million and was the world's largest restaurant chain. The company served over 22 million customers every day from 12 000 restaurants, one-third of which were owned directly with the other two thirds being franchised. Company expenditure on TV advertising was over US$ 1 billion in 1991.[1]

Although the company operated across the world, the majority of its restaurant units were in the USA and Canada: 76 per cent at the end of December 1991.[1] Outside the US, Europe was the fastest growing source of revenue during the 1980s, as can be seen in Figure 14.1.

In the early 1990s, McDonalds started opening restaurants in Eastern Europe: by summer 1992, for example, two had opened in Prague, Czech Republic and three in Budapest, Hungary. By comparison, there were some 90 McDonalds in London, England, at that time.

---

* This case has been based on published data and private survey information. © Copyright Aldersgate Consultancy Limited 1993.

Change in global sales profile

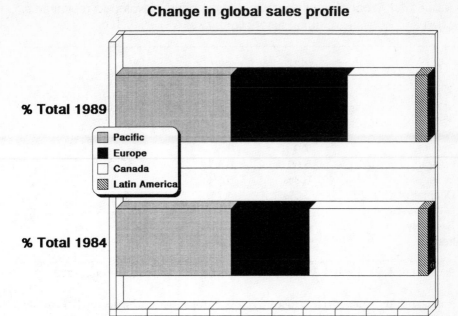

Figure 14.1 McDonalds' turnover outside the USA

EUROPEAN RESTAURANT MARKET

For reasons of history, climate, culture, wealth and national tastes, the eating-out experience across the European Community (EC) is varied and the industry fragmented. Statistics on EC market size and growth in these circumstances have only limited meaning. As Table 14.1 shows, Europe's wealthiest countries, France and Germany, spend lower proportions of their income on eating out than some poorer countries. Two of Europe's poorer countries in terms of wealth per head, Spain and Ireland, are at the opposite ends of the same spectrum.

The EC restaurant industry is equally difficult to characterise. Some individual countries have recognisable distinctiveness:

- fish and chip shops in the UK;
- bierkeller in Germany;
- tapas bars in Spain.

These have been exported on a limited basis to other EC countries in order to provide interesting new eating experiences and a reminder of past holidays. But the

Table 14.1 Proportion of household expenditure devoted to restaurants, cafes and hotels (excluding alcoholic drinks)

	1987	1980
Spain	14.0%	11.2%
UK	12.8%	12.2%
Italy	9.8%	8.1%
Portugal	9.7%	9.4%
Belgium	7.9%	7.5%
France	6.6%	6.4%
Greece	6.3%	5.3%
Denmark	5.5%	4.7%
Netherlands	4.9%	4.7%
Germany	4.4%	4.6%
Ireland	1.9%	1.5%

Source: Eurostats (1991) *A Social Portrait of Europe*, OPOCE, Luxembourg, p 128

general market competitive structure across Europe is characterised by low market share, limited branding and little pan-European activity.[2]

McDonalds Restaurants opened its first outlets in Europe in the late 1970s. In some countries, Wimpy hamburger and Kentucky Fried Chicken outlets had already been established. But none of these had the heavy TV advertising and single-minded standardisation of McDonalds. With some caution in the early years, the company then developed a chain of restaurants that set new standards in fast food operation.

McDONALDS: THE DRIVE FOR STANDARDISATION

The McDonalds 'Big Mac' double hamburger with cheese has become so standardised around the world that a price survey of this product in different countries has been used regularly by *The Economist* magazine to compare buying power in different countries.[3]

McDonalds' founder, Ray Krok, was convinced that his vision of a consistent quality, value-for-money menu worldwide would appeal to increasingly global tastes. It was this approach that was introduced across Europe during the 1980s and into Eastern Europe at the turn of the decade. It included:

- the big 'M' red and yellow branded symbol;

- 'Ronald McDonald' clown featuring in heavy TV advertising and in-restaurant activity;

- key town centre locations often at high rental cost;

- standardised decor, lighting, food and cooking and service equipment often costing as much as US$750 000 per site;

- standardised food products such as the trade marked 'Big Mac' double hamburger with cheese and 'Chicken McNuggets' coated chicken pieces.

To achieve the necessary standardisation, the company also invested heavily in the development and maintenance of its quality of supplies, speed of preparation and friendly restaurant service. It was recognised early on that so much of this depends not on centralised mass production but team and individual effort at each individual restaurant location. Among the innovations were the setting up of McDonalds 'Hamburger Universities' to train and motivate staff to the same high standards worldwide. There are now four such training institutions in the USA, UK, Germany and Japan.

McDONALDS CUSTOMERS

McDonalds Restaurants have usually commenced by targeting families with children: the 'Ronald McDonald' clown character, the menu range and some of the promotional activity have all been developed for this group.

Because most of the European restaurants are in town centre locations, many customers are likely to be shoppers, office workers and, in some towns, tourists. In the evening, customers will also extend to those who are visiting cinemas and other evening entertainment. The US drive-in fast food outlet located on major highways has still to arrive in any quantity in Europe.

THE McDONALDS MARKETING MIX

To provide further detail on the McDonalds marketing mix, a survey was carried out in late August and early September 1992 at McDonalds Restaurants in selected major European cities. I munched my way across Europe, ordering and eating a sample meal in each location: 'Big Mac, medium French fries and a medium diet coke, please'. The cooked product, its price in local currency, any promotional offers and the overall restaurant presentation were all recorded at the time.

The results of the survey are described in the remaining sections of this case. The important issue explored concerns the standardisation described above: to what extent is the McDonalds marketing mix truly standardised?

McDonalds marketing mix: product

While the menu range is partially standardised, the company itself has always recognised that customers' tastes have developed differently on a national basis across Europe:

- Norwegian McDonalds customers are served with MacLaks, a form of salmon sandwich well known in Norway;

- Swiss customers are given a choice of red or white wine or beer along with their 'Big Mac'.

In the survey undertaken and shown in Table 14.2, it was established that McDonalds have adapted their menu range to suit national tastes in Western Europe to a limited extent. The two Eastern European restaurants visited had a limited standard menu: this was possibly for logistical reasons (difficulty in obtaining ingredients), as well as scale (only three restaurants in Budapest, two in Prague) and market positioning (a local, spicy goulash might not enhance the global image in the early days of the new chain).

Table 14.2 McDonalds marketing mix: product

	Variations in menu range	Variation of food cooking and service from standard
Glasgow, Scotland	Breakfast menu	Big Mac heavy with lettuce and onion, no gherkin
London, England	Breakfast menu	Slow service: over 4-minute wait in line
Amsterdam, Netherlands	French fries served with optional mayonnaise	More coke, less ice cubes than UK
Vienna, Austria	Salad range and vegetarian burger. All burgers served in cardboard box (not polystyrene)	Big Mac cool. No ice cubes in coke
Prague, Czech Republic	No diet coke. Limited menu range. No medium French fries	Big Mac had only limited vegetables. Superb French fries: best in sample
Luxembourg	'Chinese week' special menu items. Burger served in cardboard box	French fries looked pale and were soft
Budapest, Hungary	No diet coke. No medium French fries	Big Mac cool. Some black sections on French fries. No top for drink carton
Berlin, Germany	'Chinese week' special menu items. Burger served in cardboard box	French fries variable: some well cooked, some not. Salty

In addition to the menu range offered, there is another important element in product marketing in McDonalds: the service element. Each restaurant has an individual responsibility to produce the menu range according to the cooking standards taught at the Hamburger University. This aspect of services marketing is often separated out into three extra elements: people, physical evidence and process.[4] However, for brevity, it is included in this survey under the 'product' category.

Table 14.2 shows that, in terms of service, there was more variability. While all the food was perfectly palatable, there were significant variations in quality: hence the importance of the Prague French fries, which were easily the best in the sample. It is my guess that in this case the high quality was probably connected with the fact that the restaurant had only been opened earlier in the week, and the company had probably imported and trained new management for the occasion.

McDonalds marketing mix: price

The survey prices for the standard meal were gathered across Europe and are shown in Table 14.3. It should be noted that the currency translation values were

Table 14.3 McDonalds marketing mix: price

	Currency and conversion rate to £ sterling	Prices Big Mac*	Medium French Fries	Medium diet coke
Glasgow	£ sterling	1.74	0.80	0.66
London	£ sterling	1.74	0.80	0.66
Amsterdam	Dutch gilder £1 = G3.00	5.45	1.95	2.75
Vienna	Austrian schilling £1 = AS19.4	33	16	15
Prague	Czech Koruna £1 = Kcz50	48	19 [large size]	47
Luxembourg	Luxembourg francs £1 = LF56	97	45	47
Budapest	Hungarian forints £1 = Ft140	135	74	49
Berlin	Deutsche-mark £1 = DM2.70	4.60	2.20	2.50

*In local currency

those operating at the time of the survey: sterling was devalued two weeks later by around 10–15 per cent when it left the Exchange Rate Mechanism.

McDonalds marketing mix: promotion

In addition to advertising operating at the time, there were also a series of national promotions. These are listed in Table 14.4. All the promotions listed were operating during the last week of August or first week of September 1992.

Table 14.4 McDonalds marketing mix: promotion

	Promotion operating
Glasgow	'Funky neon cups': free children's item
London	'Low price for coke and burger' promotion price offer to generate sales
Amsterdam	Coupons for price reductions at local tourist attractions
Vienna	Salad promotion via price reduction
Prague	None: new opening so most activity concentrated on explaining restaurant and generating customers via leaflets etc
Luxembourg	'Chinese week' menu promotion
Budapest	None
Berlin	'Chinese week' promotion

McDONALDS AND THE SINGLE EUROPE

In early 1993, the McDonalds European Communications director, Martin Campiche, was quoted as saying that for the company the single Europe was largely meaningless.[5] He pointed out that McDonalds selected its local franchise holders in each country and used local suppliers. Advertising and promotions were also handled on a national basis. As a result, there was little cross-border trade and, in this sense, lowering tariff barriers and removing customs controls would make little difference to the company's activities. The company hardly traded across borders.

CASE QUESTIONS

1. Examining the arguments for standardisation and the actual product variations in each country, do you think McDonalds have achieved the right balance? Or is more standardisation across Europe required?

2. Where was the best value for money in Europe? What factors beyond currency will influence the country price variations found in the survey?

3. Are there any circumstances where you would recommend a standardised promotion across Europe for McDonalds? What are they? Why?

4. Is McDonalds truly pan-European in its approach to marketing? Or do you agree with the communications director that a pan-European approach is largely meaningless?

REFERENCES

1. McDonalds Restaurants Annual Company Report and Accounts 1991.
2. European Commission (1991) *Panorama of EC Industry 1991/92*, OPOCE, Luxembourg, pp 24–9 to 24–17.
3. See, for example, 'Big Mac Currencies Again', *Economist*, 17 April 1993, p 101.
4. Booms, B H and Bittner, M J (1981) 'Marketing strategies and organisation structures for service firms' in J Donnelly and W R George (eds) *Marketing of Services*, American Marketing Association, Chicago, pp 47–51.
5. Buckley, N. (1993) 'Only Ronald strides the frontier', *Financial Times*, 4 January, p 8.

15

Marketing organisation for Electrolux 'white goods' business[*]

Electrolux is one of the world's leading producers of domestic electrical appliances such as vacuum cleaners, washing machines, refrigerators and microwave ovens. Sales in 1990 were US$5424 million, making it the largest in Europe. Its international headquarters is in Sweden but it has 43 factories in Europe and the USA.[1] Its leading US subsidiary trades as the Frigidaire Company.[2]

In the 20 years to 1990, the company grew rapidly by the acquisition of national domestic appliance companies in a number of European and US countries.[2] As a consequence, the company bought some companies that had strong and proud national traditions in manufacturing and marketing such products, and some well-known brand names. The European marketing and production structure described in the case needs to be seen in this historic context.

For reasons of clarity, the case concentrates on part of the domestic appliances business, ie the Electrolux refrigerators and freezers operation. This is often called the 'white goods' business in the industry. The other parts of the Electrolux domestic appliances business are considered only briefly in the text.

The primary focus of the case is on European marketing. However, one of the main roles for marketing is to interface with production. This is therefore also covered in the organisation structure.

Ultimately, you may regard the Electrolux organisation as being either over-complex for its task or, alternatively, as being essential to manage complex European and global marketing issues, even if some changes were needed.

BACKGROUND TO MARKETING STRUCTURE

As mentioned above, the 20 years to 1990 were a period of consolidation in the global domestic appliances industry. The leading companies discontinued some famous brand names after acquisition. Others were simply continued as a 'badge'

---

[*] This case has been prepared from published data sources only. © Copyright Aldersgate Consultancy Limited 1993.

for their own products. Some of the leading names that Electrolux consolidated in this way are shown in Table 15.1.

Table 15.1 Electrolux consolidation of brand names

1970	1980	1988	1990
Electrolux Arthur Martin Husqvarna Vest-Frost Zankar Eureka Tappan	Electrolux		
Zanussi Corbero Thorn Domar	Zanussi Corbero Thorn Domar	Electrolux	Electrolux
Athens Stove White-Westing Gibson Franklin Kelvinator Frigidaire Hamilton	WCI		
D&M	D&M Buderus	Buderus	

Note: Not all names disappeared. Some were kept as 'badges' for products that were made to standard international designs in order to maintain national customer loyalty.

Source: Company accounts

The basic reason for the disappearance of some names was the Electrolux drive for the advantages of pan-European and global operations, eg:

- production economies of scale;

- research and development budgets of sufficient size in global terms;

- global branding of major appliances.

Electrolux international organisation was then set up to handle the resulting group of companies.

ELECTROLUX 'WHITE GOODS' ORGANISATION STRUCTURE

Much of the work was devolved from the lean headquarters in Sweden to the individual country business units, of which there were some 500. Each unit produced a profit and loss account, and balance sheet on a regular basis, so that it was relatively easy for the headquarters to monitor progress against agreed plans.

By 1989, the basic structure that had evolved for the group's 'white goods' operation is shown in Figure 15.1. The organisation structure also reflects another aspect of management thinking: it was the Electrolux management's view was that there was benefit in having some in-built competition between the various parts of its marketing and production organisation across Europe and the USA.[3] The resulting conflicts of interest and responsibility are described below.

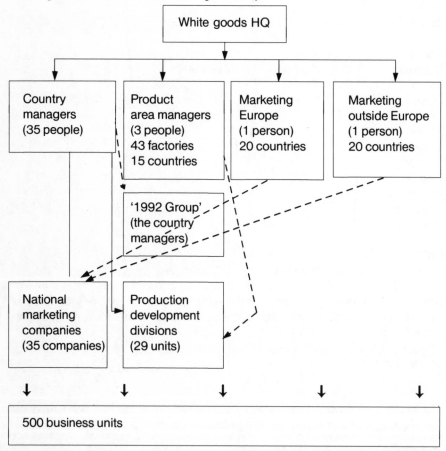

Figure 15.1 Electrolux organisation for its white goods operation

The main elements of the organisation structure for the 'white goods' operation were as follows.

1. *Headquarters* in Sweden. A small and lean team that monitored individual business units by product and business against the agreed plans.

2. *Country managers* in most individual countries. They had responsibility for the whole of their country's operations, and specifically were responsible for successful management of the balance sheet, and profit and loss statement for that country.

    Their responsibilities were then sub-divided into the business units that were reported back to Sweden by country and product, eg refrigerators in France, freezers in France.

    Their main task was to exert real management pressure on the production and sales companies in their countries to achieve the agreed objectives. They also often handled large retail customers, such as country retail electrical shop chains, and conducted wage and salary negotiations with the workers and trade unions.

3. *1992 Group* met on an occasional basis, as required, and consisted of the country managers. Its objective was to coordinate and manage all areas of product development strategy, especially from an international perspective.

    The group gave the country managers a perspective beyond their own countries and was intended to overcome increasing criticism of the country bias in the organisation: some senior managers judged that national responsibilities were not appropriate for the new Europe and for global trends.

4. *Product area managers* worked out of headquarters in Sweden. They were responsible for coordinating product development and manufacturing (but not marketing: see below). They were very senior in the organisation.

    There was only one worldwide in the white goods area. The manager responsible spent much of the time travelling.

5. *Marketing manager Europe* also worked out of Sweden. Responsibility was for marketing coordination across Europe. Specifically in Europe, two brand ranges had been identified for further consolidation: Electrolux and Zanussi. The manager had particular responsibilities in this area.

6. *Marketing manager outside Europe* similar to the above but for a different geographical area.

7. *Product development divisions* were responsible for product development and production from, at most, two factories usually in the same country. The divisions were allocated international responsibility for a small group of products that were not duplicated elsewhere. This rule was applied rigorously when Zanussi joined Electrolux in 1984, and led to some major reallocations of factories between Italy, France and Scandinavia.

    The divisions dealt with marketing companies at arm's length and had 'total freedom' to negotiate transfer prices. The divisions also had partial responsibility for product planning in order to expose the factories to market place pressures.

8. *Marketing and sales companies* had national responsibility for marketing and

sales. They negotiated with the product divisions and also with Electrolux customers.

In theory, the arm's-length relationship allowed the marketing and sales companies to purchase product from product divisions in other countries. In practice, this caused tension with the country managers to whom they reported: the profit was consolidated into the national accounts of the country from whom the purchase had been made so their own country managers lost out on the profit contribution.

9. *Business units*   were responsible for a product in a particular country. There were some 500 of these units in the company.

IMPLICATIONS OF THE ORGANISATION STRUCTURE

The main difficulty was that it was not clear who took the main management decisions about the business.[3] Electrolux was not just operating a matrix structure[4] which might typically have:

*   international product group managers;

*   national country managers responsible for all products in that country.

Electrolux had also seperated the production and sales/marketing units within countries: these were not necessarily coordinated. Moreover, the country production units were also given a seperate, decentralised global responsibility for a product or range. Both country production and country marketing/sales were then coupled with product area managers and marketing area managers that overlooked the whole process and had responsibility for coordination.

The result was that there was some uncertainty. Managers of companies that were acquired who had been used to a more hierarchical structure sometimes became upset by this ambiguity. They were told that they either had to live with it or leave the company.[3]

There also had to be extensive informal communication across the company to overcome these difficulties. Managers had to feel able to make open, informal and frequent contact with other colleagues to overcome the issues that arose. Not all managers felt comfortable in these circumstances.[3]

Another issue with the organisation structure was that there were some tensions almost built into the organisation:

*   between production divisions and marketing companies;

*   between both of these and the country managers;

*   between the country managers and the product area managers;

*   between the country managers and the marketing area managers.

Over the years, the country managers had, in practice, obtained a significant amount of power, which they appeared to wield with vigour. They had a reputation for being tough and primarily concerned for their own area of business which included sales and profits, regardless of where the products were manufactured. Since they also had responsibility for a specific product area of the group as well, this could lead to conflicts of interest.

There were some senior Electrolux managers who felt that the days of the country manager were over: they were no longer appropriate for pan-European activity. However, the head of the white goods division felt that they were good at their jobs. Moreover, there were still important national responsibilities that needed to be tackled. With all the inter-relationships of international white goods manufacture coupled with most sales still being made on a national basis, he was keen to continue with country managers.

CASE QUESTIONS

1. What would you recommend? Should the white goods division continue with country managers?

2. If the country managers were to be discontinued, how could this be done, yet still retaining their experience and management skills? What would be the new organisation structure?

3. If the country managers were retained, how would you resolve the conflicts that existed? Or would you make no changes at all?

REFERENCES

1. Electrolux Company Annual Report 1990.
2. Electrolux Company Annual Report 1991.
3. Lorenz, C (1989) 'An impossible organisation but the only one that works', *Financial Times*, 21 June, p 14.
4. Lynch, R (1992) *European Marketing*, Kogan Page, London, p 227.

16

The CMB packaging merger*

In spring 1989, two major companies, Carnaud (France) and Metal Box (UK), announced that they were merging their packaging interests to make what they claimed to be the largest packaging group in Europe and the third largest in the world. The objective was to take advantage of the new opportunities brought about by the single Europe. It was to be undertaken through a merger between two equal partners, rather than an acquisition of one by the other.

In reality, there were a number of problems that would make it difficult to realise the benefits of the single Europe: not least among these were the strong competition existing in the European packaging industry and the proudly independent traditions of the two companies being merged. This case describes the business background to the merger and explores the way the two companies were combined together in the period 1989–90.

Specifically, it raises questions in two marketing and strategy areas.

1. Is it possible to obtain the benefits of the single European market without a radical restructuring of two companies when they are being brought together? If so, how should this be undertaken?

2. To what extent do mergers between companies rooted in different countries need to develop a corporate culture based on a new view of European customers? If this is necessary, how might it be developed?

BUSINESS BACKGROUND: THE EUROPEAN PACKAGING MARKET

In 1989, the European packaging market was worth over ECU40 billion[1] and possibly as much as ECU130 billion, depending on precisely what is included in the definition of 'packaging'. Market growth in the 1980s was also imprecise, but it was typically in excess of price inflation in many parts of Europe and possibly as high as 10 per cent pa in some markets. As can be seen from Table 16.1, there were many raw materials that could be used to provide packaging. The choice for customers depended on:

---

* This case has been prepared from published data sources only. © Copyright Aldersgate Consultancy Limited 1993.

- the cost of the chosen form;

- the objective of the packaging, eg preservation of jam versus storage and display of cosmetics;

- new innovations in packaging in both of the above areas.

Table 16.1 Source of raw materials for European packaging

	as % of total market
Glass	7
Paper/card	30
Plastics	30
Light metal, eg aluminium	16
Heavy metal, eg steel	4
Wood	4
Other	9
Total	100

Source: European Commission, *Panorama of EC Industry 1991/2*, pp 6-7

While packaging for some products was traditional, eg wine in bottles, customers of the packaging manufacturers were able to make substantial sales gains by seeking packaging innovation, eg packing wine into long-life boxes. Much of this innovation in the years from 1960 came from new technology that allowed glass/cans/plastic packaging materials to be used increasingly to substitute for each other. This greatly increased the potential for competition in the European packaging industry.

Most of the top European packaging companies also manufactured other products besides packaging, eg St Gobain (France) made glass car windows as well as being the largest producer of glass containers in Europe, Stora (Sweden) not only made cardboard packaging but was also the largest producer of paper and pulp products in Europe. Since many companies do not publish this information of their sales, it is not possible to quantify the extent of European company direct involvement in packaging. However, the leading companies with significant involvement are shown in Table 16.2.

EUROPEAN PACKAGING BUSINESS STRATEGY

The critical success factors governing profitability in European packaging were largely the same areas as those that had led to a great increase in takeovers and mergers in the industry in the period 1988–90. They can be summarised as follows.

1. *Economies of scale* were significant: it was easy to spend US$1 billion on new paper mill.[2] However, there were some limitations: transport costs were a significant part of metal canning costs, thus limiting the geographical range that could be served by one factory.

Table 16.2 Turnover of European packaging companies

		Sales $US million	
Pechiney	France	12.0	metal
Stora/Fedlmuehle	Sweden	5.0	paper
SCA/Reedpack	Swe/UK	4.1	paper
St Gobain	France	4.0	paper
WTA/Arjomari	UK/France	3.9	paper
Tetrapak	Sweden	3.7	plastic paper
Modo	Sweden	2.7	paper
CMB Group	UK/France	2.4	metal
Ball Corporation	US	2.2	metal
Smurfit	Ireland	2.2	paper

Note: the above includes non-packaging turnover for the companies listed.

Source: Company reports

2. *Market strength* in terms of market share and geographic coverage were associated not only with scale economies but also with pan-European customers.[3] Leading soft drinks companies sought supplies across national boundaries and prices that reflected the resulting order size.

3. *Distribution strength*: packaging manufacturers regularly controlled their own merchants and distributors. Up to 40 per cent of their turnover might come from this source, especially in the paper and glass packaging industries.[4]

4. *High research and development costs*: these would benefit from spreading over as large a turnover as possible. Innovations in the packaging market typically cost millions of ECU.[5] Product innovation was vital for the larger companies.

5. *Move into higher added value products*: there was a trend away from 'commodity' products like cheaper papers, standard clear glass and and the associated commodity price fluctuations in raw materials such as paper pulp.[5,6]

While the precise circumstances of a merger will vary with the companies involved, many of the above factors were important in explaining the benefits envisaged by the merger of Carnaud and Metal Box in 1989. Clearly, they needed to be reflected in the business strategies to be adopted by the merged company.

THE TWO COMPANIES

Carnaud history and management style

The French Carnaud company was founded in the 1920s from the tinplate business of the Wendel family: it had long been involved in the French steel industry. The family's interests were later sold to the French investment group C.G.I.P.

(Compagnie Generale D'industrie et de Participation) and these included the Carnaud company.

By the early 1980s, Carnaud had started to incur significant losses. The former diplomat and anglophile chairman of CGIP, M Ernest-Antoine Seilliere, recruited a new chairman and chief executive in 1983 for Carnaud, M Jean-Marie Descarpentries. At the time of the merger with Metal Box, he was still very much in charge of Carnaud.

The career background of M Descarpentries is a classic example of the progression of a member of the French élite management group. He was a graduate of the highly prestigious Ecole Polytechnique and, after national service in the French paratroops, he joined France's leading glass-making company, St Gobain. This company had a reputation as a management training ground for French senior managers and provided him with his first major business experience.

In 1983, the still young M Descarpentries joined Carnaud. He immediately set about dynamising people in the company by devolving responsibility to individual managers and giving them objectives. To undertake this, the company was split into smaller managerial companies, each responsible for its own profits. This meant devolving financial responsibility as well: for example, by the early 1990s, there were some 33 banks responsible across France for the affairs of individual Carnaud companies.[7] The devolved nature of Carnaud made consolidation of the accounts slow and laborious, but it allowed the chief executive to hold each company fully responsible for the achievement of agreed objectives.

As a result of this reorganisation, the company became profitable during the 1980s. It also benefited from the personal management style of M Descarpentries: a balance between Gallic flare and entreprenurial skills, coupled with his close personal involvement as a French 'patron' with a wide personal knowledge of and influence in all his company's businesses. He claimed that it was possible to run the Carnaud company 'on the telephone' without formal procedures.[8]

In 1989, Carnaud's interest in combining with Metal Box rested on its enthusiasm for the opportunities of the single Europe together with access to Metal Box's well-respected research facility. This simply did not exist in the French company's devolved operations, but was important for product innovation in European packaging.

Metal Box history and management style

Metal Box had a strong share of the UK market for metal cans. This was the case both for food products, where demand was relatively static, and for beverages, which was still growing rapidly. Its UK share had been built over many years, and was based on a single-minded determination to offer service and value for money that would not be beaten by competitors.

In management style, Metal Box was centralised and slow to change. For example, its concentration on metal packaging meant that the rapid developments in plastic packaging for food, eg for dairy desserts and yogurt, and for cosmetics, eg lipsticks, in the 1960s and 1970s were largely missed by the company. For many years, it saw itself in the metal canning industry rather than more broadly in the packaging industry.[9] By the late 1970s, Metal Box began to invest more heavily in plastic packaging research and development (R&D), such that by the early 1990s 90 per cent of its R&D budget was on plastics, in spite of 90 per cent of its turnover being in metal canning.[7] But the company believed that this was the advantage of a centralised company: it could pursue identified opportunities with single-minded vision.

The Metal Box chairman, Brian Smith, was a firm believer in the merger with Carnaud. However, he was much older than M Descarpentries and, although he was a member of the management board after the merger, he retired after one year. Another leading Metal Box manager, Mr Murray Stuart, also joined the merged CMB board on its formation in 1989, but he subsequently left the company in 1990. Alex Watson from Metal Box then took over in 1990 as the senior UK manager in the merged group.

Metal Box saw the prime benefit of the merger as being customer-related: the packaging industry was becoming more global. It was essential to be able to offer multinational customers like Coca-Cola (US) worldwide deals on can pricing, and this implied a scale of operation beyond the UK and at least into Europe.

It should be noted that soon after setting up its part of CMB, the UK parent of Metal Box decided to shift its UK strategy. It acquired the UK company Caradon, whose main business was in bathroom equipment. However, the UK parent retained its share in CMB (see below for details) and said that it had no desire to sell. This still remained the case in 1991.

THE MERGER

When the two companies came together in 1989, it was presented as an example of how to create a 'truly European company' to match the increasingly global competition of Japanese and US companies.[10] Precisely which Japanese packaging companies were supposed to be active in Europe was never explained so there may be some rhetoric in this statement.

Importantly, both companies recognised that they had previously been rivals in European markets, though even after the merger they only had 6 per cent of the European packaging between them.[9] Since they were roughly of equal size in terms of turnover, it was resolved that the parent companies would take equal shareholdings in the newly merged company, as shown in Table 16.3.

Table 16.3 Shareholding in the merged CMB

CGIP	France	25.5%
MB Group	UK	25.5%
Outside shareholding	various	49.0%

The new company was quoted on the Paris Bourse and London Stock Exchange. The shares were priced at 2500p soon after the merger. They fell to 1800p in January/February 1990, but recovered to 2150p by May 1990.

First financial results from the merger

Early financial results of the merger are summarised in Table 16.4. The profit before tax actually dropped in the year after the merger. This was partly due to extraordinary costs associated with a reduction of 2500 in the workforce of 36 000.

Table 16.4 Financial results of the merger to 1990

CMB Group results to 31 December (million FF)	1990	1989
Turnover	24 415	21 316
Trading profits	1 413	1 481
add exceptional profits	164	1
less financial expenses	726	553
Profit before tax	851	929
Net assets: total assets less current liabilities	18 421	N/A
Turnover details:		
Metal packaging	17 182	N/A
Plastic packaging	4 850	
Other	2 383	
Total	24 415	
France	6 336	
UK	7 241	
Rest of Europe	7 555	
Other	3 283	
Total	24 415	

Source: Company accounts

While previous turnover figures were not available, it would appear from the 1990 data that the merger had largely consolidated the sales from the existing companies: there was no major shift over the first year in the group's global business. Twenty-six percent of sales were from France, 30 per cent from the UK and 31 per cent from the rest of Europe.

Newly merged organisation

M Jean-Marie Descarpentries was chosen as the new chief executive of the CMB Group. He immediately set out on four major policy initiatives, which we will examine in turn:

1. to put the customer first;

2. to give the organisation, especially the UK part, a more entrepreneurial and less centralised structure;

3. to ensure that senior managers were held accountable for the businesses under their control;

4. to develop a new European culture for the company.

Putting the customer first

The new chief executive explained his concept by describing the new policy as being like an inverted pyramid with the customers at the top and the general management at the bottom reporting to the shareholders.[10] This is shown in Figure 16.1.

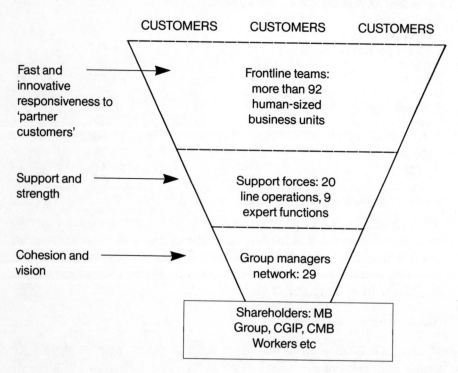

A COMMUNITY OF ENTREPRENEURS

CUSTOMERS   CUSTOMERS   CUSTOMERS

Fast and innovative responsiveness to 'partner customers' → Frontline teams: more than 92 human-sized business units

Support and strength → Support forces: 20 line operations, 9 expert functions

Cohesion and vision → Group managers network: 29

Shareholders: MB Group, CGIP, CMB Workers etc

Figure 16.1 The CMB inverted pyramid

To drive home the point, when he took his senior executives on a team-building exercise to Jordan in 1990, a group photograph was taken at the ruined city of Petra. It showed the 29 executives standing on the steps of the palace holding hands to symbolise a united company. They stood in the shape of an inverted pyramid to illustrate the shape of the company.

More decentralised structure

As was already known from his actions in the French company, the new chief executive believed in a highly decentralised organisation. Individual business units were set up based on product and geographic lines. These were in turn part of a network of plants in the same business sector.

Since the French part of CMB was already organised in this way, M Descarpentries concentrated on the former UK part. He observed that it was much more centralised and he therefore proceeded to reorganise it into smaller units. It should be reported that some UK managers resented this. They felt that he was reducing CMB into small, weaker units so he could exert his dominance over them.[10]

After one year, he had organised the group into 29 units. This was later split further into 50 units, all organised along geographic and product lines. Because this new group was larger than his former French company, he acknowledged that it would be necessary to introduce more formal procedures for major decision making. However, no major changes in this area had been made by mid-1990.[8]

Management accountability

The new chief executive said that his aim was to create 'a community of entrepreneurs'.[10] To do this, he instituted a system that made managers accountable for certain financial criteria in their units: each unit was then subject to scrutiny on such criteria as operating margins, productivity and working capital usage. Low performers were identified and urged to reach the standard of the average.

To make what he saw as a key shift in group thinking, the chief executive adopted an openly confrontational personal style with individual managers. He did not hesitate to make profit comparisons between units and placed managers into two camps: routine managers or real entrepreneurs.[10]

New culture

M Descarpentries was determined to forge a new culture. It would be neither Franco-British nor Anglo-French but European. He moved the company headquarters to Brussels. He also took managers away on team-building exercises and restructured the group as described above.

He had turned round the Carnaud group from loss to profit in France in the mid-1980s. He was now determined to use similar methods in the CMB Group to create a new thriving organisation that was truly able to take advantage of the opportunities opened up by the single Europe.

CASE QUESTIONS

1. What were the main reasons in favour of the merger of the two companies? Were these reasons consistent with the critical success factors identified for business strategy in the European packaging industry?

2. What reorganisation did CMB then set in operation? Why? How did this new structure relate to the identified trend in the market place of dealing with increasingly global customers?

3. What were the main elements of the new European culture of the company? How were they to be implemented?

4. What problems, if any, were caused by the two majority owners having equal shareholdings? Would there have been any advantages in having one dominant partner? And disadvantages?

5. Overall, in spite of some obvious early problems, do you judge the moves made in the first two years to have been a good beginning for the merger?

REFERENCES

1. European Commission, *Panorama of EC Industry 1991/92*, OPOCE, Luxembourg, p 6–7.
2. Thornhill, J (1990) 'Paperchase: the quest for optimum size', *Financial Times* 29 January.
3. Urry, M and Taylor, R (1990) 'Reedpack bought for £1.05 Bn by Swedish paper company', *Financial Times*, 21 June.
4. Dawkins, W and Leadbetter, C (1990) 'People in glass houses start to throw stones', *Financial Times*, 8 May.
5. Leadbetter, C (1991) 'Arjo Wiggins Appleton to buy leading German papermaker', *Financial Times*, 6 August.
6. Taylor, R (1990) 'Stora builds its muscle in the Community', *Financial Times*, 30 April.
7. Thornhill, J (1992) 'Partners reap the fruits of reconciliation', *Financial Times*, 15 September, p 24.
8. Urry, M (1990) 'A marriage showing first signs of strain', *Financial Times*, 15 May, p 25.
9. Author's own experience dealing with Metal Box when working on aseptic packaging at Kraft General Foods in the period to 1977.
10. Thornhill, J and Dawkins, W (1991) 'A troubled marriage', *Financial Times*, 13 September.

Appendix
Populations of some
European countries

European Community	Millions 1991
Germany	79.7
Italy	57.7
United Kingdom	57.4
France	56.9
Spain	39.0
Netherlands	15.0
Greece	10.2
Belgium	10.0
Portugal	9.9
Denmark	5.1
Ireland	3.5
Luxembourg	0.4

European Free Trade Area	
Sweden	8.6
Austria	7.8
Switzerland	6.7
Finland	5.0
Norway	4.2
Iceland	0.3

Eastern Europe	
Russia	149.8
Ukraine	52.5
Poland	37.9
Yugoslavia	23.7
Romania	23.2
Czech Republic	10.4

Slovak Republic	5.3
Hungary	10.6
Belarus	10.4
Bulgaria	9.0
Azerbaijan	7.2
Georgia	5.5
Moldova	4.4
Lithuania	3.8
Armenia	3.3
Albania	3.0
Latvia	2.7
Estonia	1.6

Index

Note: the words 'Europe' or 'European' are excluded unless they form part of the title of an organisation. For example, the European car market is indexed under 'cars and trucks' while the European Commission is listed under its full title.